CSS ANIMATIONS AND TRANSITIONS

for the Modern Web

STEVEN BRADLEY

 PEACHPIT PRESS

CSS Animations and Transitions for the Modern Web
Steven Bradley

Copyright © 2015 Steven Bradley Glicksman

Adobe Press books are published by Peachpit, a division of Pearson Education.

For the latest on Adobe Press books, go to www.adobepress.com. To report errors, please send a note to errata@peachpit.com.

Acquisitions Editor: Victor Gavenda
Development Editor: Robyn G. Thomas
Production Editor: David Van Ness
Technical Editors: Virginia DeBolt and Terry Noel
Copyeditor: Robyn G. Thomas
Proofreader: Liz Welch
Compositor: Danielle Foster
Indexer: Rebecca Plunkett
Cover and Interior Design: Mimi Heft

Printed and bound in the United States of America

ISBN-13: 978-0-133-98050-9
ISBN-10:   0-133-98050-2

9 8 7 6 5 4 3 2 1

Acknowledgments

This book is the work of many people. I'd like to thank the fine people at Adobe Press. Thank you Victor, Robyn, David, Virginia, and Terry. Many more people, who I'll never know, have had a hand in producing this book—thank you.

I'd also like to thank my family and friends for their general support and encouragement. Thank you, Mom, Dad, David, H, and Kristine.

About the Author

 Steven Bradley is a freelance web designer and WordPress developer who traded the hustle and bustle of his origins in New York for the blue skies and mountains of Boulder, Colorado. He's the author of *Design Fundamentals: Elements, Attributes, & Principles,* which is available as an ebook at www.vanseodesign.com/downloads/learn-design-fundamentals.

In addition to designing and developing websites, he blogs regularly at Vanseo Design (www.vanseodesign.com/blog) and runs a small business forum (www.small-business-forum.net) to help freelancers and entrepreneurs get started on their journey.

When not working, Steve can be found playing softball on a nice evening or reading on a rainy day. He enjoys hiking the trails of Colorado's mountains and is curious about everything.

Table of Contents

Getting Started

CSS continues to evolve as a language, and as it does it gives us a greater ability to create with code. Transforms, transitions, and CSS animations are good examples of things we could create only in graphics and animation editors. The file size of a few lines of code is measured in bytes. The size of a file containing a moving graphic is measured in megabytes and requires an additional request to the server. For the sake of performance, look first to doing things with code.

The recent design trend has been to remove signals of depth and other details used to mimic realistic objects on the screen. Unfortunately, some of those details also serve a purpose in communicating information in websites and web apps. Motion is replacing depth as the way to communicate what's been removed and adding back delight in a way that's more in tune with the fluid and dynamic nature of the web.

This book will start you on your path to adding motion to your designs. It will show you how to work with transforms, transitions, and CSS animations in modern browsers, and it will show you how to make changes to CSS properties over time instead of instantly.

The basics covered in this book will help you understand how to create more realistic animation and present some practical examples you can apply to the websites you design and develop.

What's Inside This Book

Animation is about showing changes over time. We'll look at some of the things we can change, namely CSS transforms. Transforms give us the ability to modify things like the size and position of an element. They do this in a way that doesn't interrupt the document flow. In other words, when the element changes, other elements on the page don't react. They treat the transformed element as though it were still in the original state.

Most changes to the elements of a website happen instantly. Mouse over a button, and it immediately changes color. Mouse out, and the color reverts back, again instantly. Changes that happen instantaneously aren't very realistic, which is where transitions come in. We'll use transitions to alter the time over which these changes occur so they appear more natural. Subtle changes will add a touch of realism and not be so jarring.

Transitions have a couple of limitations. First, they occur in response to some action, such as hovering over an element. We can't initiate a transition without some interaction by a site visitor. Second, you have only a single starting point and a single end point.

CSS animation isn't bound by either of these limitations. You can set an animation to start on its own (or in response to user action). Using keyframes, you can add as many or as few points between the beginning and end where you can make additional changes.

At times, you'll want to use transitions and at other times you'll prefer animation. I'll mention some of these throughout the book.

Once you understand how to work with transforms, transitions, and animations, and have some idea when to use them in real-world projects, we'll take a look at the real world again and think about how you can make your animation more realistic.

A Note About Images and Examples

One limitation of print is that it's static. We won't be able to show actual transitions and animations in this book. The figures in this book show before, after, and during moments and describe the movement.

However, every example presented in this book has a corresponding live example, which you can download, experiment with, and use. Each example is identified by number in the text, and you can view each in action as a demo to see what's being discussed or as a way to double-check your code.

How to Download Code and Example Files

Along with the examples, you'll be able to download all the code used in this book.

1. Go to www.peachpit.com/register and create or log in to your account.

2. Enter the book's ISBN (978-0-133-98050-9), and click Submit.

3. On the My Registered Products tab of your account, you should see this book listed.

Who Is This Book For?

We assume that you've picked up this book because you're interested in learning about animating web pages. You should already know how to build web pages and websites. You might be new to web design, or perhaps you've been developing websites for years. As long as you can create an HTML document and know how to work with CSS, you'll be able to follow along and work through the examples.

Knowing—or at least being able to read—JavaScript will be helpful, although not necessary. Some of the examples in this book use JavaScript to read and modify the CSS properties of some HTML elements. The scripts are short and not too difficult to understand. I'll explain each when you encounter them.

Most importantly, you should use your imagination. You can combine the things you learn in this book in multiple ways to create a variety of effects. I can show you only so many in one book. I'll point you to resources for more examples, but you'll get the most from this book if you experiment on your own and see what effects you can create.

How Do You Use This Book?

We designed this book to be used in a couple of ways. Naturally you should read through the text as you would any book. The text will present new information and help you understand it. Just as important are the examples accompanying the text.

You'll get more from this (or any technical book) by typing the code in a text editor. Open your favorite code editor or grab one from the list in the following section. Open a few browsers (you should have as many available as possible). Then start coding and checking to see how your code works.

Type the example code, and modify it. Typing will reinforce everything you read and will help you develop the muscle memory so you can write it on your own. Remember to use your imagination. Modify the example code, and observe what happens.

In code listings throughout the book, a single line of code onscreen might wrap to two lines in the book. If this happens, the continued line will start with an arrow, so it might look like this:

```
The beginning of the code starts here,
→ but it continues on this line.
```

Code that you should type or modify or that you should pay particular attention to appears highlighted.

```
-webkit-transform: translateY(0px) scale(1,1);
   -ms-transform: translateY(0px) scale(1,1);
       transform: translateY(0px) scale(1,1);
```

You'll find step-by-step instructions to show you how to complete a process. Note that instruction appears as the numbered step, and a description follows it, like this:

1. Add a `div` to your HTML with a class of `ball` and wrap another `div` with a class of `stage` around it.

   ```
   <div class="stage">
       <div class="ball"></div>
   </div>
   ```

   The reason for the `.stage div` is to provide a frame for the animation. Because you and I are probably looking at browsers open to different widths and heights, it would be hard to use the browser's edge as the thing the ball bounces against. By creating a stage for the ball, we can including it in the animation and make it more likely we're both seeing the same thing.

Each example that has a matching file containing all the code is identified in the text:

We'll get to those functions momentarily, but for now let's take a look at a simple example showing a transform (**EXAMPLE 2.1**).

Tools Required

Although tools like Adobe's Edge Animate or Tumult's Hype 2 can create animation for us, we won't be using them in this book. We won't be using Photoshop or Maya or any other tool that can create movement. These are all great tools, but we're going to create movement by writing code.

That means that the tool requirements are minimal and you should already have everything you need. You'll need a code editor, a modern browser, and working knowledge of HTML and CSS. Oh, and bring your imagination.

If you build websites with any regularity, you probably have a favorite code editor, and you're free to use it. In the following sections, you'll find a few you can try if you don't yet have a favorite or just want to try a few new ones. All the editors listed can be downloaded and used for free.

I'll be using Adobe Brackets (http://brackets.io). This is an Adobe book after all, but that's not the only reason for using it. Brackets is free and open source under an MIT license.

Brackets isn't limited to running on a single platform. It works on Windows, Mac, and Linux, so if you switch operating systems between home and work, you can still use it. It has some additional features such as live reload, so you don't have to keep refreshing your browser to see the effect of your changes.

Brackets can be extended and already has an active community building extensions for it. Brackets is built using the same technologies you use to develop websites. It's built with HTML, CSS, and JavaScript, so you may not need to wait for someone else to develop an extension. You probably have all the skills needed to create it yourself.

Brackets isn't your only choice. The following sections list free editors that you can use regardless of which platform you use and some specific to an operating system.

Universal

◆ Brackets: http://brackets.io

◆ jEdit: www.jedit.org

◆ Komodo Edit: http://komodoide.com/komodo-edit

◆ KompoZer: http://kompozer.net

◆ Sublime Text: www.sublimetext.com (free if you don't mind a little nagging)

◆ Aptana Studio: www.aptana.com/products/studio3

◆ Eclipse: www.eclipse.org

◆ Emacs: www.gnu.org/software/emacs

◆ Vim: www.vim.org

◆ Bluefish: http://bluefish.openoffice.nl/index.html

OS X

◆ Text Wrangler: www.barebones.com/products/textwrangler

◆ SubEthaEdit: www.codingmonkeys.de/subethaedit

Windows

- Notepad++: http://notepad-plus-plus.org

- EditPad Lite: www.editpadlite.com

- HTMLKit: www.chami.com/html-kit

Linux

- Gedit: https://wiki.gnome.org/Apps/Gedit

- Kate: http://kate-editor.org

CHAPTER 1

INTRODUCTION

Not long after people began designing web pages, they looked for ways to make static HTML elements more dynamic. Designers change background colors when hovering over an element or hide and show content when an element is clicked. We've known since the early days of the web that the pages we designed could do more than display statically.

Many of the changes we've wanted to include have required JavaScript, which is fine if you know JavaScript, but what if you don't? What if your skills include HTML and CSS but don't include programming?

You're in luck. With HTML and CSS alone you can make quite a few changes to how your design elements look or where they're located on the page without any programming. Best of all, you're going to learn how by reading this book.

Design Layers

Designing a positive experience on your website has several layers:

◆ Functional—First and foremost your design needs to be functional. You're building it for a purpose, and it has some functional requirements to meet before it can be considered a working website.

 The function might be as simple as presenting articles to be read, or it might be as complex as selling hundreds or thousands of products through an ecommerce system. Before anything else, your site has to work.

◆ Reliable—Assuming your site is functional, it needs to be reliable. It can't function only here and there. It should meet its functional needs always. The site should be stable and have consistent performance.

◆ Usable—Next on the list is making the site usable. It's all well and good if your site is working reliably, but if no one can understand how to use it, what does it matter? Visitors to the site shouldn't have to work too hard to find the content they want or complete a purchase.

◆ Proficient—You don't have to dumb down your design. You likely have users of different skill sets and experience. What a less savvy user finds easy, a power user might find slow and in the way. A good design helps make all users more proficient. It should help lead beginners who want to learn more down the path of becoming expert, and it should get out of the way of the experts.

◆ Creative—This is the layer on top of everything. It's the layer where aesthetics rule. It's where you can make a design beautiful. This is the layer that delights and wows, and it's probably the one viewers will remember most. This is the layer where you can connect emotionally with your audience and share the personality of the site and the people behind it.

FIGURE 1.1 summarizes these layers.

All these layers contribute to the user experience. The more of these that you can get right, the more that people will enjoy using your design, tell others about it, and recommend it.

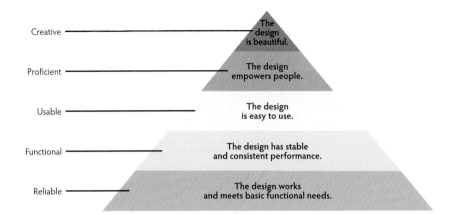

FIGURE 1.1
The hierarchy of
design needs

Animation

Where does animation fit? It won't make your site functional or more reliable, but it can contribute to the creative, proficient, and usable layers—the three layers on top. You can easily see how animation adds to the creative layer and how it can delight audiences. Who doesn't enjoy well-done animation?

What might not be as easy to see is how animation can make a site more usable and help users become more proficient. Animation can show instead of tell. Subtle movements can offer feedback that lets viewers know when they've done something correctly and when they haven't. It's an attention-getting, visual cue that leads users through a design and indicates where they can go next to learn more.

Movement is simply one more element you can use to improve the design of a website. It might be just another design element, but it's one that can do quite a lot. Adding movement to a design

◆ Grabs attention

◆ Adds polish

◆ Wows visitors

◆ Adds personality

◆ Keeps visitors more engaged

◆ Creates a memorable and lasting impression

- Connects with visitors emotionally

- Provides feedback

- Allows for interaction

- Creates a sense of realism

- Indicates changes over time

- Build stronger relationships with an audience

- Provides another layer of information

If a picture is worth 1000 words, what's a moving picture worth? 1000 pictures? Animation communicates more, and it communicates more quickly, saving your visitors time. Something they'll no doubt appreciate. While words and picture can communicate similar information, people will more likely watch a short animation than read a lengthy piece of text.

Graphic design is fundamentally about telling a story. It's about communication. Animation shows change over time and helps tell your story through that layer of time. Animation can make sequences and connections clearer and can help create a narrative flow.

Great! Animation can do a lot.

It's also likely to become the next trend in web design. If you look back at the list of things that movement can add to a site, you might realize that movement is not the only way to add them. Designers have many other ways to grab attention, create realism, and wow an audience.

For years, designers have been using depth cues to make their designs more realistic. Drop shadows, textures, and gradients help mimic real-world objects. For a while these things delighted us and impressed us the same way a realistic painting might delight and impress.

However, two problems were lying in wait:

- Designers took it too far. When used in moderation, depth cues did everything animation could do. Unfortunately, designers weren't good at the moderation part. Realism was overdone to the point where it stopped delighting and starting annoying.

◆   Mimicking real-world objects doesn't take advantage of what the web can
    do. Designers were treating the web as a static, printable document. The
    web is fluid. It's dynamic. The way something looks at one moment doesn't
    have to be the way it looks a moment later. We weren't playing to the web's
    strengths; we were playing to its weaknesses.

These problems contributed to the recent trend toward flat design. We became
so saturated with depth and skeuomorphic realism that web designers did a
complete 180 and removed what had become little more than ornamenta-
tion—designs became flat.

In the last couple of years, many of the details we had been relying on to
communicate have been removed. It's given the web a fresh look, but it's also
reduced the effectiveness of our communication to some degree. The details
we removed were providing visual cues that helped make sites usable.

I've no doubt that depth cues will return. They're useful. I hope when they do
they'll be more subtle. Until then, animation will fill the gap.

Transitions

Changes over time are going to be the next trend and that means we'll be transforming design elements through subtle transitions and keyframe animation.
It's already starting.

◆   Information slides in from the left and right as you scroll down a page.

◆   Buttons pulse to draw attention or provide feedback to users.

◆   Background colors change not in an instant but over a few milliseconds.

◆   Progress indicators show continuous progress.

◆   Diagrams and infographics are interactive.

Skillful designers are creating longer animations to illustrate difficult concepts
and engage us in ways that static pictures can't. I call it a trend, but I expect
it'll last long beyond the trend stage. Movement is coming, and it's here to stay.

We have to be careful. It's just as easy to overdo animation and movement as it
was depth. Movement attracts attention, but if every part of your site is moving at the same time in an effort to attract attention, nothing really stands out.

I want to offer one last reason for learning to work with animation. It's just plain fun. By the time you finish this book, I hope you'll see how relatively easy it is to set up some simple transitions and animation and how rewarding and enjoyable it is to see your code come to life in a browser. Remember the first time you wrote some HTML and a little CSS and then checked a browser to see what you'd done? Well, this is like that except better. Before, you placed things on a web page. Now you'll move them around.

Why Transitions and CSS Animation?

I've been talking about animation as though it's one thing. However, there are different kinds of animation and different ways to create them. When you hear the word animation, you might think of Disney movies or Looney Toons and Hanna-Barbera cartoons of your youth. Maybe you think of SpongeBob or Bugs Bunny or Anime.

They are one kind of animation, and the techniques in this book can be used to create something similar online. I don't know that you'd want to code a two-hour animated movie, but I suppose you could. However, if you did, many tools could do this efficiently and effectively—you work visually, and the tool produces the code. Tools don't always produce the most performant code, though. They often leave behind bloat. For simpler animations that you use on a website, the better choice is to write your own code.

The animation we're talking about here will be far more subtle with simple changes over time. Animation doesn't have to be a full-length movie or a 10-minute cartoon. It can be a small and subtle change to a link when you hover over it. We'll be more concerned with these smaller changes over short durations of time throughout this book, although by the time we're finished, you will have the knowledge to create far more.

Not only are there different types of animation, there are different ways to create them. Designers have been working to add movement to web pages since there were web pages. At first it was dynamic HTML or DHTML, which was a fancy way of saying "let's add JavaScript so stuff on the page can change." It wasn't always easy, because browsers were far more limited back then.

Today's libraries, such as jQuery, make animating with JavaScript easier, but some of these libraries can be very large and include much more than we need.

We've used Flash, which looked great, but it was slow to load and often inaccessible. Flash content isn't seen by search engines, and it requires plug-ins to run. Flash also doesn't work by default with today's touch devices like smartphones and tablets.

Scalable Vector Graphics, WebGL, and HTML Canvas are also technologies that you can use in the creation of animation, but these aren't quite as ready as we'd like, and they are a little harder to work with at the moment.

We'll be sticking with something you already know, CSS. We'll use CSS to transform elements, and we'll use CSS to transition these transformations as well as a number of other CSS properties over time. We'll then build on what we learn to create keyframe animations that allow more granular control over both the changes and the time over which they change.

This will lead to smaller files and less HTTP requests, and best of all, it's easy to learn. You already know how to code CSS. What's learning a few more properties? We'll use transitions and animations in a way to enhance our designs progressively. Our code will also be easy to modify, letting us quickly alter the animation or create something new.

We're going to add back some of the wow we've taken away as we've moved toward flat designs. Our animations won't be mission critical, but they'll be fun.

Browser Support/Polyfills

One question about the latest and greatest web technologies is whether or not browsers support them. We're in luck. Browser support is very good for transforms, transitions, and animations. It's not perfect, but it's very good. Where support isn't present, JavaScript polyfills can help you mimic the unsupported CSS.

The latest versions of all modern browsers support 2-dimensional transforms (**FIGURE 1.2**). You'll need to use vendor prefixes for some older versions, and you'll need to use a polyfill to make them work in Internet Explorer 8 and earlier. IE9 and earlier don't support 3-dimensional transforms, and you'll need to do a little extra work to make them work in IE10 and IE11 (**FIGURE 1.3**).

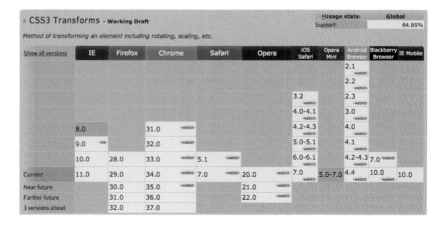

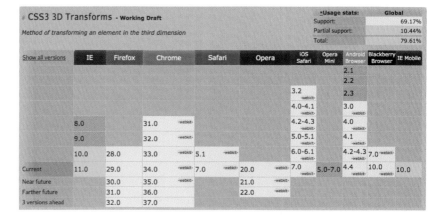

Support for transitions (**FIGURE 1.4**) is similar. Once again, you'll need to use vendor prefixes for some browser versions, and IE9 and earlier don't support transitions. A polyfill doesn't exist that you can use, but you do have some clear trending to consider. Both IE9 and IE8 are being used less and less each month. IE9 will fall away quicker as no version of Windows calls IE9 the best version to use. IE8 might stick around a little longer because it's the end of the XP upgrade path. You'll have to think about whether you need to support these versions at all, and you'll have to use transitions in a way that won't break your web pages in case you do need to support them.

# CSS3 Transitions - Working Draft	IE	Firefox	Chrome	Safari	Opera	iOS Safari	Opera Mini	Android Browser	Blackberry Browser	IE Mobile
*Usage stats: Support — Global 81.9%										
Simple method of animating certain properties of an element										
							2.1 -webkit-			
							2.2 -webkit-			
						3.2 -webkit-	2.3 -webkit-			
						4.0-4.1 -webkit-	3.0 -webkit-			
	8.0		31.0			4.2-4.3 -webkit-	4.0 -webkit-			
	9.0		32.0			5.0-5.1 -webkit-	4.1 -webkit-			
	10.0	28.0	33.0	5.1 -webkit-		6.0-6.1 -webkit-		4.2-4.3 -webkit-	7.0 -webkit-	
Current	11.0	29.0	34.0	7.0	20.0	7.0	5.0-7.0	4.4	10.0 -webkit-	10.0
Near future		30.0	35.0		21.0					
Farther future		31.0	36.0		22.0					
3 versions ahead		32.0	37.0							

FIGURE 1.4
Browser support for CSS Transitions (http://caniuse.com/#feat=css-transitions)

The situation is exactly the same with animation (**FIGURE 1.5**) as it is for transitions. The same browsers and versions support animations, and once again you don't have a polyfill fallback. As long as you don't use animation to supply critical visual information, you'll be OK. Your fallback should be to make sure any browser that doesn't support animation will still work as intended. Users will miss out on the added things that animation and transitions bring, but your site will still function as it should.

# CSS3 Animation - Working Draft	IE	Firefox	Chrome	Safari	Opera	iOS Safari	Opera Mini	Android Browser	Blackberry Browser	IE Mobile
*Usage stats: Support 80.51% / Partial support 1.23% / Total 81.74%										
Complex method of animating certain properties of an element										
							2.1 -webkit-			
							2.2 -webkit-			
						3.2	2.3 -webkit-			
						4.0-4.1 -webkit-	3.0 -webkit-			
	8.0		31.0 -webkit-			4.2-4.3 -webkit-	4.0 -webkit-			
	9.0		32.0 -webkit-			5.0-5.1 -webkit-	4.1 -webkit-			
	10.0	28.0	33.0 -webkit-	5.1 -webkit-		6.0-6.1 -webkit-		4.2-4.3 -webkit-	7.0 -webkit-	
Current	11.0	29.0	34.0 -webkit-	7.0 -webkit-	20.0 -webkit-	7.0 -webkit-	5.0-7.0	4.4 -webkit-	10.0 -webkit-	10.0
Near future		30.0	35.0 -webkit-		21.0 -webkit-					
Farther future		31.0	36.0 -webkit-		22.0 -webkit-					
3 versions ahead		32.0	37.0 -webkit-							

FIGURE 1.5
Browser support for CSS Animation (http://caniuse.com/#feat=css-animation)

Ready to Get Started?

CSS transforms, transitions, and animation are fun to work with. There's something about seeing the results of your code move around on screen that recalls the feeling you probably had the first time you looked at a web page you developed in a browser.

All are fairly easy to understand, and with a little practice you'll find them easy to work with. Even better, you'll gain the practice you need going through this book. I've created plenty of simple and more complex examples you can use to start your own exploration.

Let's not wait any longer. Let's get started transforming HTML elements with CSS alone.

CHAPTER 2

TRANSFORMS

The CSS visual formatting model determines how elements are laid out visually in a document. Each element in the document tree generates zero, one, or more rectangular boxes according to the box model. Several things determine the layout of these boxes:

- Box dimensions
- Relationships to other elements
- Size of the viewport
- Intrinsic dimensions of media and images
- Type of box (block, inline, inline-block)
- Positioning scheme (normal flow, float, absolute, or relative position)

In time, the CSS Shapes Module will allow you to create elements with a variety of shapes, but at the moment every CSS box is a rectangle with sides parallel to either the top and bottom or left and right edges of the screen. Although you can vary the dimensions of the box and its location, once set they remain constant. The box doesn't move to the other side of the screen or change its size or shape on its own. It exists as a rectangular box right where you put it.

The CSS visual formatting model also defines a coordinate space (**FIGURE 2.1**). All elements in a document are positioned within this coordinate space, and the position and size of these elements are expressed in some dimension. The top-left corner of each element is the origin of that element with positive values moving to the right and down from the origin. Negative values are allowed and move the element up and to the left.

FIGURE 2.1
2-dimensional coordinate space

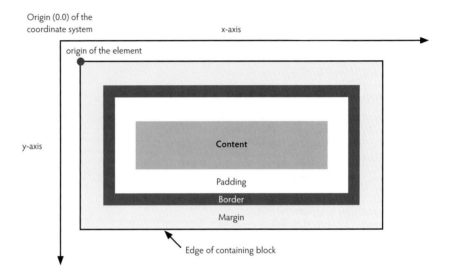

Transforms allow designers to modify the coordinate space and change the appearance of elements styled with CSS. You can translate the element to move it to a new location, rotate it, skew it, or scale it in 2-dimensional and 3-dimensional space.

Transforms offer you a way to make changes to HTML elements dynamically through CSS alone.

Browser Support and Vendor Prefixes

Browser support for 2-dimensional and 3-dimensional transforms is quite good. It's not perfect, but it's good enough that you can use transforms in production today. The browser support figures in Chapter 1 showed that many browsers still require vendor prefixes to display transforms properly.

Fortunately, not every browser needs vendor prefixes, and the majority of browser versions that do, need the same one: `-webkit`. However, IE9 needs the `-ms` prefix. That leaves Opera Mini and IE8 and below without support for 2-dimensional transforms.

We're in luck when it comes to IE. Older versions of IE support a Microsoft filter property. It works only in IE, but that's OK. A couple of JavaScript libraries do the work to convert CSS transforms to IE filters.

◆ Transformie is a lightweight JavaScript polyfill that maps transforms to IE filters (http://paulbakaus.com/2008/08/16/bringing-CSS-transform-to-internet-explorer).

◆ CSSSandpaper is a polyfill that maps transforms to filters (www.useragentman.com/blog/2010/03/09/cross-browser-CSS-transforms-even-in-ie).

Support for 3-dimensional transforms is nearly, though not quite, as good. IE9 and IE10+ don't support them, and IE10+ doesn't support the `preserve-3d` property either. Fortunately, there's a workaround, which we'll get to later in this chapter.

Before you jump on one of the polyfills, ask yourself if you really need one. The use of IE7 and below is declining. Most sites can ignore these browsers, although you should check your site analytics to be certain which browsers your visitors are using.

IE9 use is falling quickly as people upgrade to IE10 and IE11. That leaves IE8. It's the most modern browser you can get on Windows XP. Microsoft has stopped supporting XP, but people continue to use it.

Although transforms can add a lot to the design of a webpage, they should be serving non-critical functions. Your design shouldn't depend on an element rotating, for example. Your site should function whether the element rotates or not. Transforms should enhance the page and not be a critical component for the page to work.

A Word About JavaScript

The examples as written in this chapter vary a little from the example files you'll find online. To understand conceptually what's going on with transforms, I thought it would be best if you could see the before and after states of the transformation when looking at the example files in a browser. To improve them as demos, I added one or more buttons to let you turn the transformation on and off.

The buttons rely on JavaScript to work, but I didn't want to introduce JavaScript into the code in this chapter. The examples as written in this chapter won't match the source code exactly in the files. The files have a few lines of JavaScript code and use a third-party library. The code adds and removes a class named `.transformed` from the HTML element that's being transformed. The specific code to make the transform work was moved from the element to the `.transformed` class.

Follow the code as written here in the text, and view the examples in this specific chapter for a demonstration.

2-dimensional Transforms

The main property you'll use with transforms is the well-named `transform` property. It can take a value of either `none` or one of several transform functions. We'll get to those functions momentarily, but for now let's take a look at a simple example showing a transform (**EXAMPLE 2.1**).

1. Create a standard HTML document, and inside the **body** add a **div** with a class of **box**.

   ```
   <!doctype html>

   <html lang="en">

   <head>

   <title>Transform Example</title>

   <meta charset="utf-8">
   ```

```
<meta name="description" content="A simple example
→ showing how to rotate an element" />

<style>
/* We'll add our css here */
</style>
</head>

<body>
    <div class="box"></div>
</body>

</html>
```

2. In your CSS, give the **box** a **width**, **height**, and **background** color so you can see it.

```
.box {
    width: 200px;
    height: 200px;
    background: #575;
}
```

If you stop here, you'll see a medium green square on the page. Let's transform the square by rotating it 45 degrees.

3. Add the following code to your CSS to implement the rotation. Notice that I've used both the **-webkit** and **-ms** prefixes in additional to the default CSS.

```
.box {
    -webkit-transform: rotate(45deg);
        -ms-transform: rotate(45deg);
            transform: rotate(45deg);
}
```

Your **.box div** should be rotated 45 degrees (**FIGURE 2.2**).

FIGURE 2.2
Before and after rotation

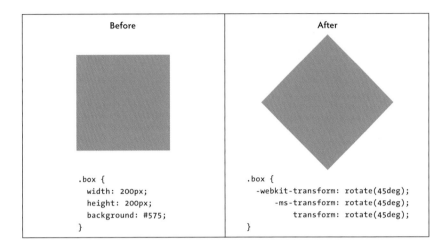

```
.box {
    width: 200px;
    height: 200px;
    background: #575;
}
```

```
.box {
    -webkit-transform: rotate(45deg);
    -ms-transform: rotate(45deg);
    transform: rotate(45deg);
}
```

Pretty easy, wouldn't you agree? Let's look at what's going on in a bit more detail. First you created a **div** with a class of **box**. You styled the **box** to give it a **height**, **width**, and **background** color so you could see it on the page. None of this should be new to you.

To transform the box, you use a named transform property and the associated vendor prefixes. The value of the **transform** property is always a transform function. Here you used the **rotate()** function and gave the function a value of **45deg**.

There are a few more transform functions available to use, but before we get to them, there's one more property we need to cover.

transform-origin Property

The other property you can use with 2-dimensional transforms is the **transform-origin** property. This property sets a fixed point around which the transform occurs. The default value for **transform-origin** is **50% 50%**, which is the center of the object being transformed.

You aren't limited to using percent values. You can specify a length in pixels (px) or any other unit of measure. You can also use any of the following keywords:

- **top**—0% in the vertical
- **right**—100% in the horizontal
- **bottom**—100% in the vertical
- **left**—0% in the horizontal
- **center**—50% horizontal and 50% vertical

Let's expand the previous example by setting a new **transform-origin** (**EXAMPLE 2.2**).

1. Wrap **.box div** in a **.container div**. This will create a reference point to see the change in origin.

```
<div class="container">
    <div class="box"></div>
</div>
```

   You need to style the **.container** enough to see it.

2. Give it the same dimensions as the **.box**, and then add an **outline**.

```
.container {
    width: 200px;
    height: 200px;
    outline: 1px solid red;
}
```

   Now you'll change the origin by setting the **transform-origin** property.

3. Add the following to your CSS styles for the **.box div**.

```
.box {
    -webkit-transform-origin: 0 0;
        -ms-transform-origin: 0 0;
            transform-origin: 0 0;
}
```

You're moving the origin, the point around which your box will rotate. You've moved it from its center to the top-left corner of the `.box` by setting `transform-origin` to `0 0`. The first value represents the horizontal origin, and the second value represents the vertical origin.

FIGURE 2.3 shows the results of changing the value of `transform-origin`. On the left, the `.box div` rotates about the default origin, which is the center of the `.box`. On the right, the `transform-origin` coordinates are (0 0). You can see the point about which the `.box` rotates changes.

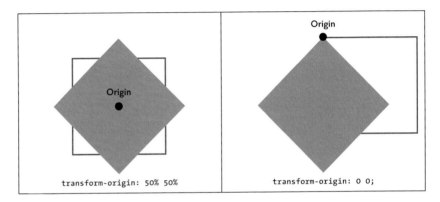

You can set the origin in any of the following ways:

- `transform-origin: left top;`
- `transform-origin: top left;`
- `transform-origin: 0% 0%;`
- `transform-origin: 0 0;`

All these options set the same origin point at the top-left corner of the element.

The `transform-origin` property isn't inherited. In other words, if you have one box inside another and you set a `transform-origin` value on the parent box, the child box still has the default `transform-origin`. You have to set it on the child if you want a new origin for child elements.

Note that the **transform-origin** property value is in relation to the bounding box of the element and not the element itself. For some elements the two will be the same, but they don't have to be. For example, let's say the **box** is a circle. You can easily set up that by giving the **box** a **border-radius** of **50%**. Adding an outline lets you see the bounding box.

4. Add the following lines of CSS to your **.box** class (**EXAMPLE 2.3**).

```
.box {
    border-radius: 50%;
    outline: 1px solid blue;
}
```

The before and after images (**FIGURE 2.4**) make it clear that the circle is still rotating around a point at the top-left corner of the bounding box and not some point on the circle.

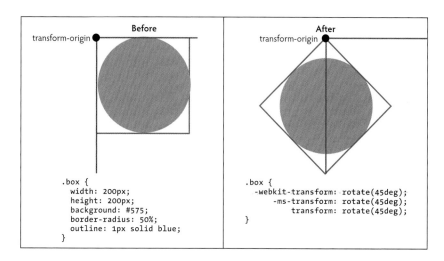

FIGURE 2.4
Rotation of the bounding box

Let's make one more change to the example. This time instead of turning the square box into a circle, you're going to add some padding and change what part of the background is painted. The latter is accomplished by setting the **background-clip** property to **content-box**, meaning only the content part of the element gets the background color.

5. Remove the **border-radius** on the **.box** class, and add the lines of high-lighted code (**EXAMPLE 2.4**).

```
.box {
    width: 200px;
    height: 200px;
    background: #575;
    outline: 1px solid blue;
    padding: 30px;
    background-clip: content-box;
}
```

Once again the before and after images (**FIGURE 2.5**) show that the origin around which the object is rotating is still the bounding box.

FIGURE 2.5
Rotation of the
bounding box

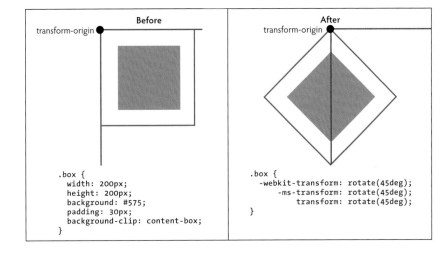

2-dimensional Transform Functions

By now you'd probably like to know how else you can transform elements other than rotating them, so let's take a look at the available 2-dimensional transform functions. **TABLE 2.1** shows all the transform functions along with examples values you might give each.

TABLE 2.1   2-DIMENSIONAL TRANSFORM FUNCTIONS

FUNCTION	EXAMPLE
translate()	translate(25%, 50px)
translateX()	translateX(5cm)
translateY()	translateX(1.75em)
scale()	scale(1.5, 0.3)
scaleX()	scaleX(4)
scaleY()	scaleY(3.25)
rotate()	rotate(45deg)
skew()	skew(30deg, 0.5rad)
skewX()	skewX(60deg)
skewY()	skewY(1.2rad)
matrix()	matrix(1, 2, 3, 5, 8, 13)

As you can see, there are four sets of named functions (**translate**, **scale**, **rotate**, and **skew**) and one **matrix** function. Let's consider each in a bit more detail—we'll save **matrix()** for the end.

translate() Function

Translating an element means moving it to a different location. You can translate elements horizontally using **translateX()**, vertically using **translateY()**, or both at the same time using **translate()**.

For example, to move an element to the right 100 pixels and down 50 pixels (**EXAMPLE 2.5**) you could specify each move with separate functions:

```
transform: translateX( 100px ) translateY( 50px );
```

Or you could set both values using a single function:

```
transform: translate( 100px, 50px );
```

Either approach leads to the same result (**FIGURE 2.6**).

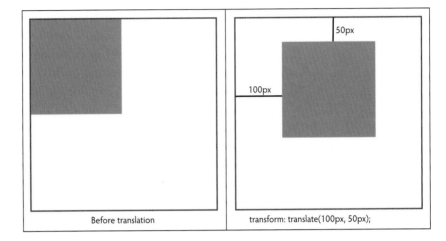

You aren't limited to using px. Any measurement will work: px, em, %, cm, and in are all acceptable. Note that when you use percentages, the measurement is a percent of the element being moved and not the element's container, which might be contrary to your first instinct.

scale() Function

Scaling an element (**EXAMPLE 2.6**) simply makes it larger or smaller. Working with the scale transform functions is similar to working with the translate transform functions. The available scale functions are **scaleX()**, **scaleY()**, and the generic **scale()**.

If you want to scale an element to twice its current size, you can specify each axis separately:

```
transform: scaleX(2) scaleY(2);
```

Or you can use a single function:

```
transform: scale(2,2);
```

The second value in the single function isn't required if it is the same as the first. You could have written:

```
transform: scale(2);
```

and still end up with the same result.

The values given to the `scale()` function should be a unit-less number—you can use decimals. For example:

```
transform: scale(1.5);
```

is valid. So is

```
transform: scale(0.5);
```

To make an element smaller, you might think you would use a negative number, but negative numbers aren't allowed. If you want to scale down something, you scale it by a value less than 1.0. In other words, `scale(0.5)` makes something half its initial size in each of the horizontal and vertical dimensions, or one fourth its overall size (**FIGURE 2.7**).

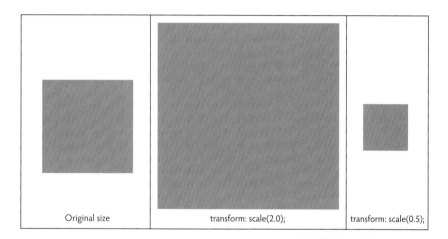

Original size   transform: scale(2.0);   transform: scale(0.5);

FIGURE 2.7
Before and after scaling

rotate() Function

We've already seen rotate in action (Figure 2.2). In 2-dimensional transforms, there are no x and y variations, which makes sense. You rotate objects around an axis perpendicular to the 2-dimensional plane. This means all 2-dimensional rotation is around an axis parallel to the z-axis.

Objects rotate around a single point, which you set with the **transform-origin** property, and by default the element rotates around its center.

`rotate()` takes an angle value: degrees (deg) or radians (rad).

```
transform: rotate(45deg);
```
```
transform: rotate(1.07rad);
```

skew() Function

To skew an object means to distort its shape. Skew behaves like translation and scaling with functions in both directions, `skewX()`, `skewY()`, as well as the generic `skew()`.

To skew an element 30 degrees horizontally and 45 degrees vertically, you can specify each with separate functions (**EXAMPLE 2.7**):

```
transform: skewX(30deg) skewY(45deg);
```

Or you can use a single function:

```
transform: skew(30deg, 45deg);
```

FIGURE 2.8 shows the results of skewing in each direction and also both directions at the same time. As with rotate, the values for the skew functions will always be an angle in units of either deg or rad.

FIGURE 2.8
Before and after skew

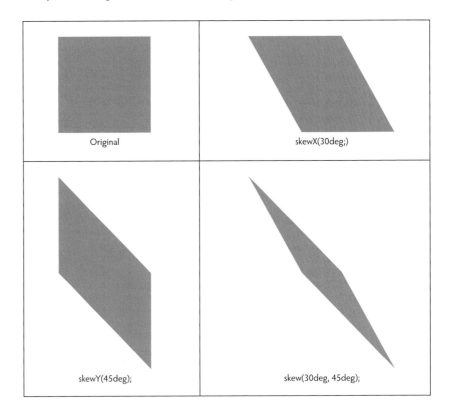

matrix() Function

Every one of the transform functions covered so far is really a specific matrix function. The named functions exist to make things easier, but they can be represented by a matrix.

A matrix is simply a rectangular array of numbers that use specific matrix math for adding, subtracting, multiplying, and dividing matrices. In computer graphics, matrices are used for linear transformations as well as projecting 3-dimensional images onto the 2-dimensional plane of the screen, which is why they come into play here.

It's been a long time since I performed matrix math. My guess is that unless you regularly use matrix math you've probably forgotten how it works, if you ever knew. Transforms deal only with matrix multiplication, so I'll skip the rest and offer a very quick explanation of how matrix multiplication works.

Don't worry. You won't need to perform any of this math in practice, although you could if you choose. I'm presenting it to demonstrate that matrices and matrix multiplication are behind the simpler transform functions.

$$\begin{bmatrix} 1 & 2 \\ 3 & 4 \end{bmatrix} * \begin{bmatrix} 5 & 6 \\ 7 & 8 \end{bmatrix} = \begin{bmatrix} 19 & 22 \\ 43 & 50 \end{bmatrix}$$

How did I arrive at the answer for this matrix? Take the first row in the first matrix, multiply each value by the corresponding values in the first column of the second matrix, and add the results of each multiplication together.

$$(1 * 5) + (2 * 7) = 19$$

This becomes the value in the first row and first column of the resulting matrix. Next, multiply the second row of the first matrix by the first column of the second matrix, and add the results. The result becomes the value that goes in the second row and first column of the resulting matrix.

$$(3 * 5) + (4 * 7) = 43$$

The math for the second column in the resulting matrix is similar.

$$(1 * 6) + (2 * 8) = 22$$

$$(3 * 6) + (4 * 8) = 50$$

That's all the math you need to know to follow what's going on—don't worry, you won't be using this math in practice. You'll probably use one of the named functions.

Remember that we're working in a coordinate system as defined by the CSS visual formatting model (Figure 2.1). The origin (0,0) in the coordinate space is at the top left. Positive values for the first value move to the right, and positive values for the second value move down a point.

When a transform is applied to an element, it creates a local coordinate system with a new origin at the center (50%, 50%) of the element being transformed. We saw this when we talked about the **transform-origin** property.

Here's how we represent a 2-dimensional transformation matrix.

$$\begin{bmatrix} a & c & e \\ b & d & f \\ 0 & 0 & 1 \end{bmatrix}$$

Since 2-dimensional transforms use only the first two rows, the matrix can be written as the vector [a,c,e,b,d,f]. A vector is a geometric quantity that has magnitude or length and a direction. For our purposes, all you need to know is that it's another way to write the matrix.

A browser applies a transform matrix by multiplying the matrix by a vector [x, y, 1], where x and y are coordinates for a point in the local coordinate space, which becomes the origin for the new coordinate space.

$$\begin{bmatrix} a & c & e \\ b & d & f \\ 0 & 0 & 1 \end{bmatrix} * \begin{bmatrix} x \\ y \\ 1 \end{bmatrix} = \begin{bmatrix} ax & + & cy & + & e \\ bx & + & dy & + & f \\ 0 & + & 0 & + & 1 \end{bmatrix}$$

or

$$\begin{bmatrix} a & c & e \\ b & d & f \\ 0 & 0 & 1 \end{bmatrix} * \begin{bmatrix} x \\ y \\ 1 \end{bmatrix} = \begin{bmatrix} ax + cy + e \\ bx + dy + f \\ 0 + 0 + 1 \end{bmatrix}$$

Again, each transform is simply a specific matrix. A translation matrix, for example, looks like the following:

$$\begin{bmatrix} 1 & 0 & tx \\ 0 & 1 & ty \\ 0 & 0 & 1 \end{bmatrix}$$

or as the scaler (1,0,0,1,tx,ty). Using the matrix, we don't specify units for tx and ty. The unit of measure is px for translation when created with a matrix.

The transform we used before to translate an element 100 pixels along the x-axis and 50 pixels along the y-axis was

```
transform: translate( 100px, 50px );
```

The same translation can be set using a matrix transformation.

```
transform: matrix( 1, 0, 0, 1, 100, 50 );
```

$$\begin{bmatrix} 1 & 0 & 100 \\ 0 & 1 & 50 \\ 0 & 0 & 1 \end{bmatrix} * \begin{bmatrix} 50 \\ 50 \\ 1 \end{bmatrix} = \begin{bmatrix} 150 \\ 100 \\ 1 \end{bmatrix}$$

All the transform functions can be written in terms of a specific matrix and used in the matrix function (**FIGURE 2.9**).

FIGURE 2.9
Transform function matrices

$$\begin{pmatrix} 1 & 0 & tx \\ 0 & 1 & ty \\ 0 & 0 & 1 \end{pmatrix} \quad \begin{pmatrix} sx & 0 & 0 \\ 0 & sy & 0 \\ 0 & 0 & 1 \end{pmatrix} \quad \begin{pmatrix} 1 & \tan(a) & 0 \\ 0 & 1 & 0 \\ 0 & 0 & 1 \end{pmatrix}$$

Translation   Scaling   SkewX

$$\begin{pmatrix} \cos(a) & -\sin(a) & 0 \\ \sin(a) & \cos(a) & 0 \\ 0 & 0 & 1 \end{pmatrix} \quad \begin{pmatrix} 1 & 0 & 0 \\ \tan(a) & 1 & 0 \\ 0 & 0 & 1 \end{pmatrix}$$

Rotation   SkewY

- Translation—[1 0 0 1 tx ty] where tx and ty are the distance (in pixels) to translate the element.

- Scaling—[sx 0 0 sy 0 0] where sx and sy units in the previous coordinate system represent one unit in the x and y directions in the new coordinate system.

- Rotation—[cos(a) sin(a) -sin(a) cos(a) 0 0]

- SkewX—[1 0 tan(a) 1 0 0]

- SkewY—[1 tan(a) 0 1 0 0]

Nested Transforms

Nesting transforms is the equivalent of applying one transform directly after another. Keep in mind that all these transforms are just mapping coordinates in one coordinate system to coordinates in a different system.

Using matrix transforms, for example, you might combine translation and scaling. Here is a translation matrix multiplied by a scaling matrix.

$$
\begin{bmatrix} 1 & 0 & tx \\ 0 & 1 & ty \\ 0 & 0 & 1 \end{bmatrix} * \begin{bmatrix} sx & 0 & 0 \\ 0 & sy & 0 \\ 0 & 0 & 1 \end{bmatrix} = \begin{bmatrix} sx & 0 & tx \\ 0 & sy & ty \\ 0 & 0 & 1 \end{bmatrix}
$$

For the combined transform, you would use the resulting matrix of the [sx 0 0 sy tx ty] vector.

$$
\begin{bmatrix} sx & 0 & tx \\ 0 & sy & ty \\ 0 & 0 & 1 \end{bmatrix} * \begin{bmatrix} 250 \\ 100 \\ 1 \end{bmatrix} = \begin{bmatrix} 250sx & + & 0 & + & tx \\ 0 & + & 100sy & + & ty \\ 0 & + & 0 & + & 1 \end{bmatrix}
$$

or

$$
\begin{bmatrix} sx & 0 & tx \\ 0 & sy & ty \\ 0 & 0 & 1 \end{bmatrix} * \begin{bmatrix} 250 \\ 100 \\ 1 \end{bmatrix} = \begin{bmatrix} 250sx + 0 + tx \\ 0 + 100sy + ty \\ 0 + 0 + 1 \end{bmatrix}
$$

Adding Multiple Transforms to an Element

I assume you'd rather not use the matrix math we just covered whenever you want to combine transforms. Fortunately, you don't have to; you can stick with the simpler transform functions.

```
transform: translate(100%, -100%) scale(2);
```

This CSS translates the element 100 percent to the right and 100 percent up, then scales the element by 2. There are two things of importance to note:

- Order matters. Matrix math is not commutative.

- There's no comma in between transform functions; you'll have to get used to omitting it.

Let's take a look at the importance of order. The following two lines of CSS do not have the same result.

```
transform: translate(100%, -100%) scale(2);
transform: scale(2) translate(100%, -100%);
```

It might seem counterintuitive, but you can work the matrix multiplication one more time, switching the order of the scale and translations matrices.

$$\begin{bmatrix} sx & 0 & 0 \\ 0 & sy & 0 \\ 0 & 0 & 1 \end{bmatrix} * \begin{bmatrix} 1 & 0 & tx \\ 0 & 1 & ty \\ 0 & 0 & 1 \end{bmatrix} = \begin{bmatrix} sx & 0 & sx*ty \\ 0 & sy & sy*ty \\ 0 & 0 & 1 \end{bmatrix}$$

$$\begin{bmatrix} 1 & 0 & tx \\ 0 & 1 & ty \\ 0 & 0 & 1 \end{bmatrix} * \begin{bmatrix} sx & 0 & 0 \\ 0 & sy & 0 \\ 0 & 0 & 1 \end{bmatrix} = \begin{bmatrix} sx & 0 & tx \\ 0 & sy & ty \\ 0 & 0 & 1 \end{bmatrix}$$

The results are different when you switch the multiplication order.

Keep in mind when nesting transform functions that you have to call all functions on the same **transform** property.

This works:

```
transform: translate(100%, -100%) scale(2);
```

This doesn't:

```
transform: translate(100%, -100%);
transform: scale(2);
```

The second example leads to the element being scaled, but not translated. If you want both, you need to assign both functions to the same `transform` property.

You can nest transforms as many levels deep as you want. The result applies the first transformation, then applies the second transformation, then the third, and so on.

The Transform Rendering Model

NOTE

If you're unfamiliar with what stacking contexts are and how they work, I've written an article explaining both, which you can find at http://webdesign.tutsplus.com/articles/what-you-may-not-know-about-the-z-index-property--webdesign-16892.

When you set a value other than **none** to the `transform` property, a new local coordinate system is established at the element where the transformation is applied. These new coordinate systems are called **stacking contexts**.

Let's take a quick look at how stacking contexts work. Each of the coordinate systems we've talked about is a 2-dimensional plane. Pretend you can grab one of those planes, and place it on top of another plane along an axis perpendicular to both planes. Think of it like stacking one piece of paper on top of another (**FIGURE 2.10**).

- Stacking context 1: Document root
  - A stacking context is like a new independent layer in your document.
  - Elements on one stacking context usually don't respond to elements on another stacking context when they render.
  - Transforms create a new stacking context, but other elements respond as though they don't when rendering.
- Stacking context 2:
  - An example is an element with a positive z-index applied.
  - The new context appears closer to the viewer.
- Stacking context 3:
  - A transform creates a new stacking context.

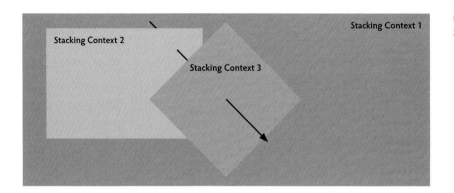

FIGURE 2.10
Stacking contexts

When a new stacking context is created as well as a new containing block for the element, it's like taking something off of one sheet of paper and moving it to a different sheet of paper.

This applies only to the display of the element and its descendants. Other elements treat the original element(s) as though they were still located on the original stacking context (the original sheet of paper).

For example, let's expand the original rotation example so it has two boxes instead of one (**EXAMPLE 2.8**).

1. Assign a class of `.box` to each **div**, and distinguish them with the additional `.one` and `.two` classes.

    ```
    <div class="box one"></div>
    <div class="box two"></div>
    ```

2. Give both **div**s the same dimensions.

    ```
    .box {
        width: 200px;
        height: 200px;
    }
    ```

3. Give each `div` its own `background` color.

```
.one {
    background: #575;
}

.two {
    background: #755;
}
```

The code results in a red square displaying directly below a green square.

4. Rotate the green square (`.one`).

```
.one {
    -webkit-transform: rotate(45deg);
      -ms-transform: rotate(45deg);
          transform: rotate(45deg);
}
```

Notice how the red square doesn't move after the green square rotates (**FIGURE 2.11**). As far as the red square is concerned, the green square hasn't changed. It still displays as it did—right where it was before the transformation. The reason is that a new stacking context was created when you applied the transform.

Even though you might transform an element by rotating it or moving it to a new location, other elements on the page act as though the element was never transformed, and the now transformed element appears to be located on top of other elements around it, making it appear closer to the viewer.

2-dimensional transforms render as a flat plane. They render on the same flat plane as their containing block. Transforming a 2-dimensional element may change how the element looks in a way so it's perceived as occupying 3-dimensional space, but it's still rendered on the same flat plane. The z-coordinate of all points on the 2-dimensional plane is 0.

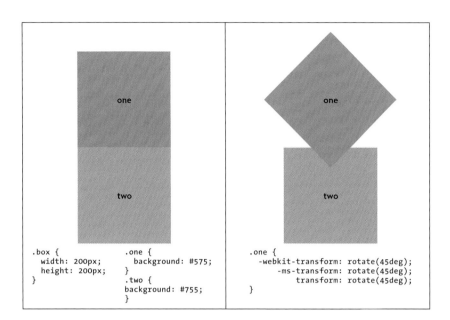

FIGURE 2.11
The transform rendering
model in action

3-dimensional transforms can have non-zero values for the z-coordinate, resulting in a transformed element being rendered on a different plane than its containing element. As you'll see momentarily, you can use the **perspective** and **perspective-origin** properties to add a feeling of depth to elements and a composition by making elements that are closer to the viewer appear larger and those farther away appear smaller.

3-dimensional Transforms

The screens that display designs are 2-dimensional. But, imagine a third dimension (the z-axis) moving into and out of the screen (**FIGURE 2.12**). You can assume the screen sits at the coordinate 0 along the z-axis and that positive values for the z-coordinate are closer to you and negative values are farther away.

Despite all this imagining, the elements are still 2-dimensional planes with 0 depth. Rectangles don't become cubes, and circles don't become cylinders.

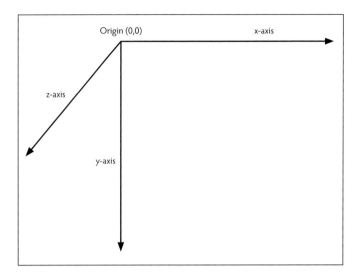

Yet by using the following additional properties, you can display elements as though they are aware of some 3-dimensional space, and they'll appear to the viewer to render in that 3-dimensional space.

*   `perspective`

*   `perspective-origin`

*   `transform-style`

*   `backface-visibility`

perspective Property

The `perspective` property is what turns on the 3-dimensional illusion. When you set it for an element, every child element inside that parent displays as though it's in 3-dimensional space. The `perspective` property takes two values: `none` or a length, with `none` being the default. Length can be any positive number or zero. While you don't specify the units, they will always be pixels. Setting `perspective` to 500 sets it to 500px even though you don't specify the px.

The smaller the length value, the deeper the perspective will be. It sounds counterintuitive, but a smaller length means deeper perspective. The value represents how far away the z=0 plane is located from the viewer. A lower value creates a flatter (more parallel to the ground) object, which creates a more pronounced perspective effect.

The best way to illustrate `perspective` is with an example. Let's use the same `.box div` we used for the 2-dimensional transform examples (**EXAMPLE 2.9**). This time we'll wrap it inside another `div` with a class of `container`.

1. Copy the file you created in the previous example, and give it a new name. Replace the HTML with the following:

```
<div class="container">

    <div class="box"></div>

</div>
```

2. Modify the `.box` class by giving it a `background` color so you can see it. Changes to the code are highlighted. You can remove the `.one` class from the previous example too if you'd like.

```
.box {

    width: 200px;

    height: 200px;

    background: #575;

}
```

3. Modify the `width` and `height` of the `.container` class and add the `perspective`. Changes and additions to the code are highlighted.

    Note that the perspective is set on the container of the element that will be transformed in 3-dimensional space and not the element itself.

> **NOTE**
>
> The value 250 in this example is arbitrary.

```
.container {

    width: 200px;

    height: 200px;

    outline: 1px solid red;

    -webkit-perspective: 250;

        -ms-perspective: 250;

            perspective: 250;

}
```

If you were to stop now, you wouldn't see much. You need to transform the `.box div` to see how it transforms itself in 3-dimensional space.

4. Rotate the `.box` around the y-axis.

```
.box {
    -webkit-transform: rotateY(60deg);
    -ms-transform: rotateY(60deg);
    transform: rotateY(60deg);
}
```

Because a **perspective** value has been set, the `.box` appears to be rotating in 3-dimensional space (**FIGURE 2.13**).

FIGURE 2.13
Rotation in 3-dimensional perspective

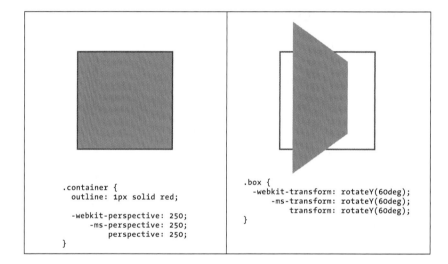

When looking at 2-dimensional transforms, you have a single **rotate()** function. You are dealing with 2-dimensional space with only one way to rotate elements, which is around an axis running perpendicular to the plane of the element—the z-axis.

Now that you're working with 3-dimensional space, you can rotate elements around any or all of the three axes. Choosing the z-axis won't do much to show perspective, though. You're better off rotating around either the x- or the y-axis. In this example, I chose the y-axis.

When working with the **perspective** property, results aren't necessarily what you expect. I gave the `.container` and `.box` divs the same dimensions in the example for a reason—to isolate the **perspective** and get results that come closer to meeting your expectations.

The best way to get a feel for how elements display in perspective is to play around with some values. I encourage you to type the previous example in your code editor, experiment with some of the **perspective** values, and observe the change in a browser. Remember, the smaller the number, the greater the perspective.

Once you have a handle on the **perspective**, try changing the values in the **transform** function. Try different rotation angles to see what happens. You can prove the **.box div** is still a 2-dimensional object by rotating it 90 degrees. It'll be perpendicular to the screen and disappear since it has no depth.

perspective-origin Property

The **perspective-origin** property is similar to the **transform-origin** property. By default, the **perspective-origin** is centered on the viewer at **50% 50%**, and like **perspective** is set on the **container** and not the transforming element.

```
-webkit-perspective-origin: 50% 50%;
   -ms-perspective-origin: 50% 50%;
       perspective-origin: 50% 50%;
```

The same values that are available for the **transform-origin** property are available with the **perspective-origin** property. Once again, you can set a percent or a length of any measurement type. You can also use the same keywords that are available for the **transform-origin** property with the same result.

- **top**—0% in the vertical
- **right**—100% in the horizontal
- **bottom**—100% in the vertical
- **left**—0% in the horizontal
- **center**—50% horizontal and 50% vertical

If only one value is specified, the second value is assumed to be center. If at least one of the values is not a keyword, then the first value represents the horizontal offset.

You're doing the same thing you did before with the `transform-origin` property: You're moving a single point around on the screen. With `transform-origin`, that point is the one around which the element transforms. With `perspective-origin`, that point represents the single point of single-point perspective.

The reason the `.container` and `.box` have the same dimensions as in the previous example is so the `perspective-origin` doesn't throw you off. If the dimensions were different, then **50% 50%** would be the center of the container and not the center of the box, which might not be what you expect. When both are the same dimensions, **50% 50%** is the center of both.

Experiment with the different values (**EXAMPLE 2.10**).

1. Add a `perspective-origin` to your `.container div` so the CSS is as follows:

```
.container {
    width: 200px;
    height: 200px;
    outline: 1px solid red;

    -webkit-perspective: 250;
        -ms-perspective: 250;
            perspective: 250;

    -webkit-perspective-origin: 50% 50%;
        -ms-perspective-origin: 50% 50%;
            perspective-origin: 50% 50%;

}
```

Nothing should change because you're using the default values for the `perspective-origin`. **FIGURE 2.14** shows the result of several different `perspective-origin`s. Try different values on your own to get a better sense of the effect of the `perspective-origin` property.

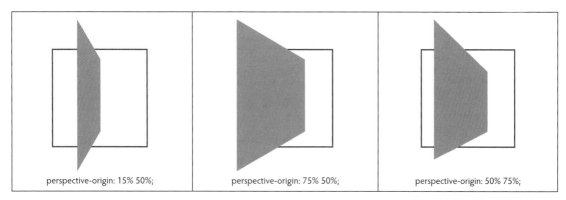

| perspective-origin: 15% 50%; | perspective-origin: 75% 50%; | perspective-origin: 50% 75%; |

FIGURE 2.14
perspective-origin

2. Adjust the first value (x-coordinate), and see how the result changes.

3. Adjust the second value (y-coordinate), and check the results.

Once you are comfortable, experiment with the dimensions for the container.

4. Increase the `.container width`. Decrease its `height`. See what happens.

Experimenting with values like this is one of the best ways to get a feel for any code.

transform-style() Property

The `transform-style` property controls whether or not the children of an element render in flat 2-dimensional space or if they render in 3-dimensional space. The `transform-style` property has only two available values: `flat` and `preserve-3d`.

```
transform-style: flat;
```

```
transform-style: preserve-3d;
```

When you set `transform-style` to `flat`, children of the element appear flattened on the parent element. When set to `preserve-3d`, they create a new stacking context and render in their own 3-dimensional space relative to the parent element. Neither affects the parent element.

NOTE

When you set `transform-style` to `preserve-3d`, other CSS can override the value. Some CSS properties require a flattened representation of an element before they can be applied. The W3C offers a list of properties and values that will override `preserve-3d`. Keep this in mind if you find your expected 3-dimensional element appearing in 2-dimensional space.

The following properties and values render an element flattened on its parent container, regardless of the value set on `transform-style` for the parent element.

- `overflow`—Any value other than `visible`

- `filter`—Any value other than `none`

- `clip`—Any value other than `auto`

- `clip-path`—Any any value other than `none`

- `isolation`—Used value of `isolate`

- `mask-image`—Any value other than `none`

- `mask-box-image-source`—Any value other than `none`

- `mix-blend-mode`—Any value other than `normal`

This is all easier to see with an example (**EXAMPLE 2.11**). Here is HTML for three nested elements: a `container`, a `parent`, and a `child`.

```
<div class="container">
    <div class="parent">
            <div class="child"></div>
    </div>
</div>
```

1. Give the `.container div` dimensions and an outline so you can see it.

2. Add values for the `perspective` and `perspective-origin` properties.

```
.container {
    width: 300px;
    height: 300px;
    outline: 1px solid red;

    -webkit-perspective: 500;
        -ms-perspective: 500;
            perspective: 500;
```

```
    -webkit-perspective-origin: 50% 50%;
        -ms-perspective-origin: 50% 50%;
            perspective-origin: 50% 50%;
}
```

3. Give `.parent div` dimensions and a **background** so you can see it.

4. Rotate the `.parent div` about the y-axis, and set the **transform-style** to **preserve-3d**. This means its children (in this case the `.child div`) render in their own 3-dimensional space.

```
.parent {
    width: 300px;
    height: 300px;
    background: #575;
    padding: 50px;

    -webkit-transform: rotateY(45deg);
        -ms-transform: rotateY(45deg);
            transform: rotateY(45deg);

    -webkit-transform-style: preserve-3d;
        -ms-transform-style: preserve-3d;
            transform-style: preserve-3d;
}
```

5. Give the `.child div` dimensions and a background color, and rotate and translate it about the x-axis and z-axis respectively.

```
.child {
    width: 200px;
    height: 200px;
    background: #557;

    -webkit-transform: rotateX(30deg)
    ⇥   translateZ(75px) translateY(40px);
```

```
        -ms-transform: rotateX(30deg)
     → translateZ(75px) translateY(40px);

        transform: rotateX(30deg)
     → translateZ(75px) translateY(40px);

}
```

FIGURE 2.15 show the results. You can see that both the .parent and .child divs render in their own 3-dimensional space. The .parent is rotated 45 degrees around the y-axis of the .container div, and the child is both rotated and translated around the .parent div's axis.

FIGURE 2.15
transform-style with
preserve-3d (left) and
flat (right)

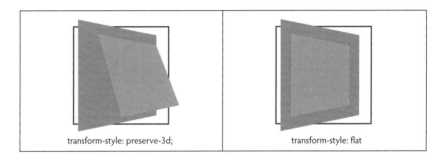

transform-style: preserve-3d;   transform-style: flat

If you change the value of **transform-style** on the parent from **preserve-3d** to **flat**, the .child div no longer renders in its own 3-dimensional space. Instead, it renders flat on the .parent as if the .child wasn't rotated or translated.

The beginning of this chapter mentioned that IE10+ doesn't currently support **preserve-3d**. I also mentioned there was a workaround, and it happens to come directly from Microsoft (http://msdn.microsoft.com/en-us/library/ie/hh673529%28v=vs.85%29.aspx#the_ms_transform_style_property).

> You can work around this by manually applying the parent element's transform to each of the child elements in addition to the child element's normal transform.

The workaround requires a bit of redundant code because you'll have to repeat CSS, but in most instances it won't be a lot; it's good to know you can still make **preserve-3d** work in IE.

backface-visibility() Property

The last property for 3-dimensional transforms is the `backface-visibility` property. The name hints at what the property does. It determines if the back side (or face) of a transformed element is visible when it's facing the viewer.

When you rotate an object 180 degrees, you expect to see the reverse side of that object. For something like a `div` filled with color, the reverse side appears the same as the front. For an element that has some text inside, the reverse side shows reversed text. The `backface-visibility` property allows you to change this. It has two available values: `visible` and `hidden`, with `visible` being the default.

```
-webkit-backface-visibility: visible | hidden;
   -ms-backface-visibility: visible | hidden;
       backface-visibility: visible | hidden;
```

Why might you want to hide the other side of an element? When you want to place two elements identical in dimensions back to back to each other. Setting the `backface-visibility` of both elements to `hidden` allows you to flip the combined object over. You can show the front of each element when it's facing the viewer and hide its back when it's flipped.

An example will make this clearer (**EXAMPLE 2.12**). Let's create a card of sorts. Each face contains a different background color and either the word front or back.

1. Here's the HTML.

    ```
    <div id="card">
        <div class="face" id="front">Front</div>
        <div class="face" id="back">Back</div>
    </div>
    ```

    The card is made up of three `div`s: one each for the front and back of the card and one that wraps the two faces. Each card face gets a class of `face`, along with an `id` to determine if the face is the front or back of the card. The card itself gets an `id` of `card`.

    Both faces as well as the card itself should be the same size, so you'll set the same dimensions on all three `div`s at the same time.

2. Set the CSS for the `color`, `text-align`, and `line-height` so the text is readable and displays in the center of the card.

```
#card,
#front,
#back {
    width: 200px;
    height: 200px;
    color: #fff;
    text-align: center;
    line-height: 200px;
}
```

You need card faces to render in 3-dimensional space so set `preserve-3d` on the `transform-style`. You also want both faces of the card to occupy the same space.

3. Use CSS positioning, and set the `#card div` to `position: relative`.

The other two lines of CSS below are cosmetic and help the example look a little better. Setting `font-size` to `2em` works well to display the text, and `margin: 1em auto` horizontally centers the card on your screen and pushes it down a bit from the top of the browser. Neither is essential to making the card work.

```
#card {
    margin: 1em auto;
    font-size: 2em;
    position: relative;

    -webkit-transform-style: preserve-3d;
       -ms-transform-style: preserve-3d;
           transform-style: preserve-3d;
}
```

4. Style each of the faces. Give both a position of **absolute** to allow them to occupy the same space. By default their top and left values are 0, which is fine so there's no need to set them. The front face is set to **red** and the back face to **blue**.

Since the back of the card should be facing away initially, it is rotated 180 degrees around the y-axis.

```
#front {
    position: absolute;
    background: red;
}

#back {
    position: absolute;
    background: blue;
    -webkit-transform: rotateY( 180deg );
        -ms-transform: rotateY( 180deg );
            transform: rotateY( 180deg );
}
```

5. Load the code in a browser.

You should see a red square in the top center of the screen with the word "Front" on it.

To flip the card, you want to rotate the **#card div** 180 degrees. However, you want to be able to rotate it back too. The way this is done is by assigning this rotation to a class and then adding and removing the class dynamically. The class is named **flipped**, since whenever it's applied, the card will be in the flipped position.

6. Create the `.flipped` class.

```
.flipped {
    -webkit-transform: rotateY( 180deg );
        -ms-transform: rotateY( 180deg );
            transform: rotateY( 180deg );
}
```

```
<div id="card"> <!-- initial state -->
<div id="card" class="flipped"> <!-- flipped state -->
```

7. Load the code in a browser.

You'll notice one problem. In the flipped state, you aren't seeing the back face of the card. Instead you're seeing the front face with the word "Front" reversed. This is where the **backface-visibility** property comes in.

The default value for **backface-visibility** is **visible** so when you flip everything, the back side of the front card face is visible. Since it sits on top of (closer than) the back card face, you see it reversed. This is not what you want. When flipped, you want the front card face to be hidden and the back card face to show.

8. All you need to do is set **backface-visibility** to **hidden**.

```
.face {
    -webkit-backface-visibility: hidden;
        -ms-backface-visibility: hidden;
            backface-visibility: hidden;
}
```

9. Load the code in a browser.

You should now see the back card face (when the `.flipped` class is added to #card) (**FIGURE 2.16**). In the live Example 2.12, I added another button and some JavaScript to toggle the **backface-visibility** property between **visible** and **hidden**.

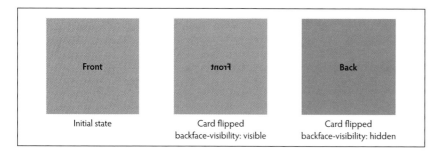

FIGURE 2.16
The effect of
different values of
`backface-visibility`

Here's the complete code for this example (including buttons and JavaScript), which you can also find online (see "Getting Started") in the files for this book.

A Word About the Asterisk

The full code example contains the following extra code:

```
* {
    box-sizing: border-box;
    font-family: helvetica;
}
```

The asterisk (*) is a universal selector, and any property set on it will affect every element in your document. `box-sizing: border-box` adjusts how a browser renders the box model. If you're unfamiliar with the `box-sizing` property, you can read more about it at www.paulirish.com/2012/box-sizing-border-box-ftw. The main reason `box-sizing: border-box` is useful is that you won't have to continue to adjust the `width` and `height` of elements when you adjust their padding or margin.

```
<!doctype html>
<html lang="en">
<head>
<title>Backface Visibility</title>

<meta charset="utf-8">

<script>
```

```
// ========= DOM Utility Functions from PastryKit
→ ========= //

// Sure, we could use jQuery or XUI for these,

// but these are concise and will work with plain
→ vanilla JS

Element.prototype.hasClassName = function (a) {
    return new RegExp("(?:^|\\s+)" + a + "(?:\\s+|$)").
    → test(this.className);
};

Element.prototype.addClassName = function (a) {
    if (!this.hasClassName(a)) {
        this.className = [this.className, a].join(" ");
    }
};

Element.prototype.removeClassName = function (b) {
    if (this.hasClassName(b)) {
        var a = this.className;
        this.className = a.replace(new RegExp
        → ("(?:^|\\s+)" + b + "(?:\\s+|$)", "g"), " ");
    }
};

Element.prototype.toggleClassName = function (a) {
    this[this.hasClassName(a) ? "removeClassName" :
    →"addClassName"](a);
};
// ========= End DOM Utility Functions from PastryKit
→ ========= //


var init = function() {
```

```
    var card = document.getElementById('card');

    var front = document.getElementById('front');

    document.getElementById('flip').addEventListener(
    ↪'click', function(){

    card.toggleClassName('flipped');

    }, false);

    document.getElementById('backface').addEventListener(
    ↪'click', function(){

    front.toggleClassName('face');

    }, false);

};

window.addEventListener('DOMContentLoaded', init, false);

</script>

<style>

* {

    box-sizing: border-box;

    font-family: helvetica;

}

button {

    margin: 0 auto 2em auto;

    width: 100px;

    height: 2em;

    display: block;

}

#backface{

    width: 150px;
```

```
}

#card,
#front,
#back {
    width: 200px;
    height: 200px;
    color: #fff;
    text-align: center;
    line-height: 200px;
}

#card {
    position: relative;
    margin: 3em auto 1em auto;
    font-size: 2em;

    -webkit-transform-style: preserve-3d;
        -ms-transform-style: preserve-3d;
            transform-style: preserve-3d;
}

#front {
    position: absolute;
    background: red;
}

    #back {
    position: absolute;
    background: blue;
```

```
        -webkit-transform: rotateY( 180deg );
           -ms-transform: rotateY( 180deg );
                transform: rotateY( 180deg );
}

.flipped {
        -webkit-transform: rotateY( 180deg );
           -ms-transform: rotateY( 180deg );
                transform: rotateY( 180deg );
}

.face {
        -webkit-backface-visibility: hidden;
           -ms-backface-visibility: hidden;
                backface-visibility: hidden;
}

</style>
</head>
<body>

<div id="card">
    <div class="face" id="front">Front</div>
    <div class="face" id="back">Back</div>
</div>
<button id="flip">Flip</button>
<button id="backface">Toggle backface-visibility</button>

</body>
</html>
```

3-dimensional Transform Functions

The 3-dimensional transform functions are very similar to their 2-dimensional counterparts, with the exception of the extra dimension. **TABLE 2.2** lists them along with some example values.

TABLE 2.2 3-DIMENSIONAL TRANSFORM FUNCTIONS

FUNCTION	EXAMPLE
`matrix3d()`	`matrix3d( 1.0, 2.0, 3.0, 4.0, 5.0, 6.0, 7.0, 8.0, 9.0, 10.0, 11.0, 12.0, 13.0, 14.0, 15.0, 16.0 )`
`translate3d()`	`translate3d( 25px, 33%, 4in )`
`translateZ()`	`translateZ( 2.375em )`
`scale3d()`	`scale3d( 2.0, 4.55, 0.75 )`
`scaleZ()`	`scaleZ( 3 )`
`rotate3d()`	`rotate3d( 1.0, 2.0, 3.0, 30deg )`
`rotateX()`	`rotateX( 45deg )`
`rotateY()`	`rotateY( 1.25rad )`
`rotateZ()`	`rotateZ( 275deg )`
`perspective()`	`perspective( 100px )`

All the 3-dimensional transform function names have **3d** tacked onto the end to distinguish them from their 2-dimensional counterparts. This tells the browser to expect a third value for the z-axis.

The **translate** and **scale** functions also get new functions specific to the z-axis.

```
transform: translateZ()
transform: scaleZ()
```

In 2-dimensional space, the **rotate** function has no component for a specific axis since the only choice is to rotate around the z-axis. With 3-dimensional rotation, you now get individual functions for each axis.

```
transform: rotateX()
transform: rotateY()
transform: rotateZ()
```

The one new function is the `perspective()` function. It's a way to set the perspective of any element. Instead of using the `perspective` property that you saw earlier

```
-webkit-perspective: 500;
   -ms-perspective: 500;
       perspective: 500;
```

you can use the `perspective()` function as a value for the `transform` property. The function has the advantage that you can include it in the chain of transform functions that can be added to the `transform` property.

```
-webkit-transform: perspective(500);
   -ms-transform: perspective(500);
       transform: perspective(500);
```

Once again as a reminder, the lower the value of `perspective()`, the greater the actual perspective.

matrix3d() Function

Matrices that are 3-dimensional work the same as 2-dimensional ones, except the 3-dimensional matrices contain an extra row and extra column. Here is an example of a 3-dimensional matrix to represent the `scale3d` function. Notice how the extra row and column are the third ones. The last row in the 2-dimensional matrix becomes the last row here.

$$\begin{bmatrix} sx & 0 & 0 & 0 \\ 0 & sy & 0 & 0 \\ 0 & 0 & sy & 0 \\ 0 & 0 & 0 & 1 \end{bmatrix}$$

This matrix can also be represented in scalar form as

`matrix3d(sx, 0, 0, 0, 0, sy, 0, 0, 0, 0, sz, 0, 0, 0, 0, 1)`

The math is the same as it is for 2-dimensional matrices, except there's a little more of it due to the extra rows and columns. Since the math is essentially the same, I won't repeat the matrix multiplication. As with 2-dimensional transforms, you'll probably use one of the named functions instead.

Each of the named functions can be represented using the `matrix()` function, though the extra dimension adds complexity. Here's a sampling of equivalent `matrix3d` functions for the some 3-dimensional transform functions. Note how complicated the `rotate3d` matrix equivalent is, and be thankful you can just use the `rotate3d()` function instead.

- translation—A 3-dimensional translation with the parameters `tx`, `ty`, and `tz` is equivalent to the matrix:

$$\begin{bmatrix} 1 & 0 & 0 & tx \\ 0 & 1 & 0 & ty \\ 0 & 0 & 1 & tz \\ 0 & 0 & 0 & 1 \end{bmatrix}$$

- skew—A 2-dimensional skew-like transformation with the parameters `alpha` and `beta` is equivalent to the matrix:

$$\begin{bmatrix} 1 & \tan(\alpha) & 0 & 0 \\ \tan(\beta) & 1 & 0 & 0 \\ 0 & 0 & 1 & 0 \\ 0 & 0 & 0 & 1 \end{bmatrix}$$

- rotation—A 3-dimensional rotation with the vector [x,y,z] and the parameter `alpha` is equivalent to the matrix:

$$\begin{bmatrix} 1 - 2*(y^2+z^2)*sq & 2*(x*y*sq - z*sq) & 2*(x*y*sq + y*sc) & 0 \\ 2*(x*y*sq + z*sc) & 1 - 2*(x^2+z^2)*sq & 2*(x*y*sq - x*sq) & 0 \\ 2*(x*y*sq - y*sc) & 2*(x*y*sq + x*sc) & 1 - 2*(y^2+y^2)*sq & 0 \\ 0 & 0 & 0 & 1 \end{bmatrix}$$

Summary

In this chapter, you learned about transforming elements in 2-dimensional and 3-dimensional space. Transforms are one type of change you can make to elements and use in animation.

Browser support for both 2-dimensional and 3-dimensional transforms is quite good. You'll need a workaround for IE10+, and you'll need to include a polyfill for older versions of IE.

You can use transformations to enhance design elements, but you shouldn't rely on your transformations to communicate in your websites just yet.

A handful of properties for 2-dimensional and 3-dimensional transforms are available:

* `transform`
* `transform-origin`
* `perspective`
* `perspective-origin`
* `transform-style`
* `backface-visibility`

Of these, the `transform` property is the one you'll use most often. It takes one or more transform functions that can translate, scale, rotate, and skew elements. For 3-dimensional transforms, there's also a `perspective()` function. You can create 2-dimensional and 3-dimensional transforms using the generic `matrix()` function.

Transforms are relatively easy to work with, although at times and especially where perspective is concerned, the results of your code may not match your expectations. The best way to get a feel for what the given values of any transform function do is to copy some of the examples in this chapter and play around with the values. Isolate a single value to experiment with, change the value, and observe the results. It shouldn't take long to get results that more closely match your expectations.

Now that you know how to change elements through the various transform properties and functions, it's time to add the element of time. You want to be able to vary these transforms over time, not instantly. The first way you'll control time is with transitions, which brings us to the next chapter.

CHAPTER 3

TRANSITIONS

Changes that occur by transforming elements happen instantly. That's not very realistic. In the real world, changes occur over some duration of time, which is where transitions come in.

Transitions define how the changes we apply to elements occur over time. Through transitions, you can control the duration of the change and how the change accelerates and decelerates. You can choose to have the change occur faster at the start and slower at the end. You can choose the reverse and have the change start slower and end faster. You can choose other combinations of acceleration and deceleration.

Transitions are simple animations between two states. Because you have some control over the time it takes to go from one state to another, you can smooth the value changes of the before and after CSS properties. Instead of an element instantly moving from one side of the screen to the other, you can set a duration that produces a less jarring movement.

Animations between two states are often referred to as implicit transitions. You specify the start and end states and leave it to the browser to implicitly define all the intermediate states in between. This gives control of the animation to the browser, which allows the browser to optimize the efficiency and performance of the animation. The browser tries to minimize painting to the screen by offloading some work to the graphic processing unit (GPU). Just know that it's the browser's decision and not yours.

When working with transitions, you determine which CSS properties (from the list of capable properties) will be animated. You determine when the animation will start and how long it will last. Finally, you get to customize the acceleration curve.

Transitions don't happen on their own. They must be triggered by an action. The action can be hovering over an element or clicking it. The action can be tabbing through a form and starting a transition when a certain element gains focus. You can use any of the usual trigger events to set a transition in motion.

Like transforms, you should use transitions for non-critical experiences. If something has to work, it shouldn't rely on a transition to make it work. Think of transitions as another way to enhance the experience instead of relying on the transition for the experience. Someone visiting your site should be able to use the site even if the transitions don't work for them.

Browser Support

Browser support for transitions is similar to the support for transforms. It's not perfect, although support is better in some ways than it is for transforms. For example, most current browser versions support transitions without using vendor prefixes. Although, you'll still want to use vendor prefix for older browser versions, and you'll need to decide which browsers you want to support.

On the bright side, you can likely use only the `-webkit` vendor prefix. Both Firefox and Opera have supported transitions for long enough that you can probably skip the `-moz` and `-o` prefixes. Naturally, that decision depends on which browsers you need to support for your project. We won't be using them in this chapter, but depending on your project you may need them.

As you can probably guess, the browser holdouts are older versions of Internet Explorer and Opera Mini. IE9 and older versions don't support transitions, but as with transforms you can use a polyfill for IE. In fact, cssSandpaper (www. useragentman.com/blog/csssandpaper-a-css3-javascript-library), one of the polyfills you can use to add transform support to older versions of IE, also adds transition support.

One additional limitation is that transitions aren't supported on pseudo-elements besides the `:before` and `:after` pseudo-elements in Firefox, Chrome 26+, and IE10+, although you probably won't bump into this limitation often.

Transitions

Let's start with a simple example (**EXAMPLE 3.1**) and change the background color of an element from blue to red when we hover over it. After the example, we'll dig in to what's going on.

1. Create a new HTML page, and add a single **div** with a class of **box**. The code should look familiar.

```
<div class="container">
    <div class="box"></div>
</div>
```

The **.box div** is wrapped with a **.container div** to make it easier to center everything on the screen. It isn't necessary for the transition and exists only to improve the presentation of the demo.

2. Center the **.container div**, and give your **.box div** dimensions and a background color. I've chosen a light blue (#33f), but you can give your box any color you'd like.

```
.container{
    width: 200px;
    margin: 5em auto;
}

.box {
    width: 200px;
    height: 200px;
    background-color: #33f;
}
```

3. Now add some code to change the `background-color` on hover. I've chosen a bright red (#f33), but you can choose any color you like. Just make it something distinguishable from what you chose for the initial state of the `.box` so the change is noticeable.

```
.box:hover {

    background-color: #f33;

}
```

If you stop here, the `.box div` will change instantly from blue to red when you hover over it and change back to blue when you stop hovering. Nothing you haven't seen before. So, let's add a transition.

4. Add the following highlighted code to your CSS to your `.box` class.

```
.box {

    width: 200px;

    height: 200px;

    background-color: #33f;


    -webkit-transition: background-color 2s;

            transition: background-color 2s;


}
```

I'll explain what the transition code is doing in the next couple of sections, but for now, just look at the difference adding a transition makes.

5. Refresh your page, and hover again over the `.box div`.

The change in color isn't instant. It now takes 2 seconds, and you can see the transitional colors.

If you used the same background colors as in the example, you should notice the `.box` changing through different shades of purple before it finally settles on red when hovering. It goes through those same shades of purple in reverse order before settling on blue when removing the hover.

FIGURE 3.1 shows some of the colors produced during the transition progresses.

FIGURE 3.1
Transition of background-color from blue to red

You used **transition: background-color 2s;** to create the transition. That's actually the shorthand, which is covered later in the chapter. We'll walk through each of the individual properties before that, but you'll probably prefer to use the shorthand version most of the time. As you can tell from the code and from observing the transition in your browser, the code transitions the **background-color** property over a 2-second duration.

For fun, remove the transition from **.box**, and instead add it to **.box:hover**.

6. Change your complete CSS to look like the following (**EXAMPLE 3.2**).

```
.box {

    width: 200px;

    height: 200px;

    background-color: #33f;

}

.box:hover {

    background-color: #f33;

    -webkit-transition: background-color 2s;

        transition: background-color 2s;

}
```

7. Reload your page, and once again hover over the **.box div**.

The result is exactly as what you saw previously. The **.box** changes color from blue to red (or whatever colors you chose) over a duration of 2 seconds. It doesn't matter whether you add the transition to **.box** or **.box:hover**. Keep that in the back of your mind for a bit. I'll provide more detail about it later in the chapter.

You might also have noticed that no transforms were used in the creation of this transition. You aren't limited to using transforms when you create a transition. You can transition many, but not all, CSS properties.

OK, let's dig in a little deeper and look at the individual `transition-*` properties before returning to the shorthand.

transition-property Property

The first `transition-*` property is `transition-property`. It defines which CSS properties are transitioned in your document. It takes a list of one or more CSS properties for its values, such as `background-color`, `transform`, `font-size`, or `padding-left`. You can also use the keywords `none` or `all`, which are self-explanatory.

You might be surprised to learn that the `all` keyword is the default. In other words, without doing anything, any CSS property that can be transitioned is already set to be transitioned as soon as you create a CSS file. You can turn off that default behavior with the keyword `none`, and you can overwrite it by explicitly setting which properties are transitioned.

If you're wondering why changes in your CSS values change instantly when they're set to be transitioned, you'll find out in the next section.

You can add transitions to any and all elements, including the `:before` and `:after` pseudo-elements. You can also transition multiple CSS properties using a comma-separated list.

```
.box {
    -webkit-transition-property: background-color, width,
    → height, transform;

        transition-property: background-color, width,
        → height, transform;

}
```

If you list properties as in the sample code, and one of the properties isn't animatable, it will be ignored, but it is maintained in the list to preserve the matching to the values in other property lists in your document. If one of the other `transition-*` properties doesn't have enough comma-separated values to match those listed for the `transition-property`, it repeats the list of those other values until there are enough to map one to the other.

If the same property is listed multiple times in the list, the last occurrence will be used and the non-used property is maintained in the list to preserve matching.

Example 3.1 used the transition shorthand to set a property and a time. The property could have been set as follows:

```
transition-property: background-color;
```

You can also list multiple properties as follows:

```
transition-property: background-color, top, width,
→ transform, opacity;
```

There's no limit to how many properties you can use in the list—other than to make sure the values match with the values of the other `transition-*` properties. At some point, it might make more sense to just use the `all` keyword.

Remember that the list of transition-properties you assign to an element apply only to changes for that element. Let's expand on the example from earlier in this chapter with a new example (**EXAMPLE 3.3**).

1. Create a new HTML document, and add the following HTML:

```
<div class="container">
    <div class="box"></div>
    <div class="box2"></div>
</div>
```

It's the same HTML from the previous two examples with the exception of a second `div` with a class of `box2`.

2. Use the same CSS on the `.container div` and `.box div` that you used in the previous example. Center the `.container`, and give the `.box div` dimensions, a `background-color`, and set the same transition. On hover, change the `background-color` like before.

```css
.container{
    width: 200px;
    margin: 5em auto;
}.box {
    width: 200px;
    height: 200px;
    background-color: #33f;
    -webkit-transition: background-color 2s
            transition: background-color 2s;
}

.box:hover {
    background-color: #f33;
}
```

3. To make things simple, add the same CSS to the `.box2 div`, except leave off the transition.

```css
.box2 {
    width: 200px;
    height: 200px;
    background-color: #33f;
}

.box2:hover {
    background-color: #f33;
}
```

You end up with two identical boxes, one displaying below the other, with a transition applied only to the top one. If you hover over both boxes, you'll see the top one transition the change in `background-color`, while the bottom one changes instantly.

You assign a `transition-property` or list of them to elements the same way you assign any other property to elements. Following are some examples of different `transition-*` properties you might add to different CSS selectors.

```
div {
    transition-property: background-color;
}


div > span {
    transition-property: top, left;
}


#container {
    transition-property: all;
}


.box {
    transition-property: font-size, opacity, padding-left,
    → word-spacing, z-index;
}
```

All the properties (shown as values of the `transition-property`) in this code are valid, and any changes on those properties transition instead of changing instantly. For example, `font-size` is one of the `transition-property` values on the `.box` class. Any changes to `font-size` on the `.box` class will transition.

transition-duration Property

If all you do is set **transition-*** properties, nothing different happens when changes occur to the values of the listed properties. The default state is for all properties to be transitioned, and yet no changes transition until you do more. Why? Nothing happens because you haven't set a duration over which the transition occurs.

To set the duration, you use the **transition-duration** property, which takes a time or list of times as a value.

```
transition-duration: 2s;

transition-duration: 2000ms;

transition-duration: 2s, 3s, 10s;
```

The default value of the **transition-duration** property is **0s**, which is why changes happen instantly. Negative values for the duration are not permitted and render the declaration invalid.

If you set multiple **transition-*** properties on an element, you should set an equal amount of **transition-duration**s so properties and durations match. If you list more durations than properties, the extra **transition-duration**s are ignored. If you list fewer, the durations repeat until there's enough to match.

```
transition-property: background-color, transform, width;

transition-duration: 10s, 2s, 5s, 15s;
```

In this code, the transition over the **background-color** lasts 10 seconds, the transition over the **transform** lasts 2 seconds, and the transition over the **width** lasts 5 seconds. The 15-second duration is ignored.

```
transition-property: background-color, transform, width;

transition-duration: 10s, 2s;
```

In this second block of CSS, the transition in **background-color** and **transform** is 10 seconds and 2 seconds respectively. The durations will then start to repeat and the transition in **width** lasts 10 seconds.

You can test this yourself easily enough (**EXAMPLE 3.4**).

1. Create a new HTML document, and add the following HTML:

```
<div class="container">
    <div class="box"></div>
</div>
```

2. Add the following CSS to style it:

```
.container{
    width: 200px;
    margin: 10em auto;
}

.box {
    width: 200px;
    height: 200px;
    background-color: #33f;

    -webkit-transition-property: background-color,
    →  -webkit-transform, width;
            transition-property: background-color,
            →  transform, width;

    -webkit-transition-duration: 10s, 2s, 5s, 15s;
            transition-duration: 10s, 2s, 5s, 15s;
}

.box:hover {
    background-color: #f33;
    width: 400px;

    -webkit-transform: rotate(45deg);
        -ms-transform: rotate(45deg);
            transform: rotate(45deg);
}
```

In this code, the `.box div` has three properties that transition and four durations over which the transitions occur. As mentioned earlier the 15-second
duration is ignored, since it's not needed. You can see how the `.box` looks at
each of the three durations that apply in **FIGURE 3.2**.

FIGURE 3.2
Transitioning `background-color`, `rotation`, and
`width` over three different
durations

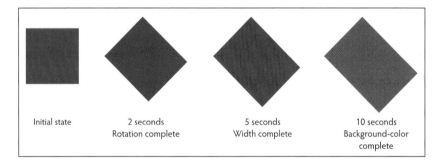

Try different numbers of values for the `transition-duration`, and observe
how long each transition occurs based on how many values you've assigned
to the property. Make sure the values of the duration are large enough that
you can tell the difference.

Matching Vendor Prefixes

One note before we move on. If you're using vendor prefixes, then all the
vendor prefixes must match. For example, Safari needs the `-webkit` vendor
prefix on the `transform` property to perform the rotation, but it doesn't
need it on the `transition-property`. However, the two have to match, so
the `-webkit-transition-property` is included even though it's no longer
necessary in the latest versions of Safari.

If you set `transition-*` properties and they aren't transitioning, check that you
don't have a mismatch in vendor prefixes between the `transition-property`
and the property you want to transition.

transition-timing-function Property

Changing something a constant amount over a set time isn't very realistic.
Typically things change speeds over time. They accelerate and decelerate at
intermediate segments in the overall duration.

The `transition-timing-function` describes how the intermediate values in a transition are calculated, and it allows for changes in speed over the duration of the transition. In other words, it allows you to accelerate and decelerate the transition at points along its duration, which helps make the animation more realistic.

These timing functions are commonly referred to as easing functions, and the two terms are sometimes used interchangeably. There are two main groups of timing functions:

* Step functions

* Cubic Bézier curves

Either type of timing function can serve as the value of the `transition-timing-function` property, and each type offers several values that you can use.

Step Functions

In step functions, the overall duration is divided into equally sized intervals. Each interval is one step closer to the final state of the element. There are three different step functions you can assign to a `timing-function`:

* `timing-function: step-start;`

* `timing-function: step-end;`

* `timing-function: steps()`

The first two values, `step-start` and `step-end`, are specific cases of the more generic `steps()` function and will be easier to understand after you've seen the generic `steps()` function.

Inside the parentheses of the `steps()` function, you add an integer to represent the number of intervals and then either `start` or `end` to tell the browser whether the change for each interval happens at the start or the end of the interval. The `start` or `end` value is optional, and if not explicitly set, it will default to `end`. An example will make this easier to understand (**EXAMPLE 3.5**).

1. Create a new HTML document, and add the following HTML:

```
<div class="container">
    <div class="box"></div>
</div>
```

2. Add some familiar CSS to give the `.box` dimensions and a `background-color`, and change the `background-color` on hover. This code uses the same blue to red that's been used throughout, but feel free to use any colors you prefer. Don't forget to center the `.container div` as well.

```
.container{
    width: 200px;
    margin: 5em auto;
}

.box {
    width: 200px;
    height: 200px;
    background-color: #33f;
}

.box:hover {
    background-color: #f33;
 }
```

3. Add the following `transition-*` properties to the `.box`:

```
.box {
        -webkit-transition-property: background-color;
            transition-property: background-color;

        -webkit-transition-duration: 5s;
            transition-duration: 5s;

        -webkit-transition-timing-function: steps(5, start);
            transition-timing-function: steps(5, start);
}
```

The transition occurs only on the **background-color** and lasts a total of 5 seconds. The **transition-timing-function** tells the browser to transition the color in five equal steps, which in this case means each step lasts one second. The **start** value in the **steps()** function tells the browser that the intermediate change should occur at the start of the interval. The transition pattern is change, interval, change, interval, until the last interval completes.

4. Test this example in a browser.

Five distinct changes (**FIGURE 3.3**) in color occur from red to blue (if you are using the same colors as the example code), which leads to several distinct shades of purple in between the starting blue and ending red. The changes happen before the interval. The first change happens instantly, and each subsequent change takes another second.

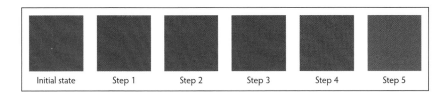

| Initial state | Step 1 | Step 2 | Step 3 | Step 4 | Step 5 |

FIGURE 3.3
Transitioning
background-color
over five distinct steps

5. Change the **timing-function** to **steps(5, end)**.

6. Test the example in a browser.

The pattern reverses. It is interval, change, and so on. But all you can probably tell is that the first change took a second, where before it was instant. Beyond that everything else looks similar.

I mentioned the **step-start** and **step-end** values being specific cases of the **steps()** function.

◆ **step-start** is equivalent to **steps(1, start)**.

◆ **step-end** is equivalent to **steps(1, end)**.

In other words, **step-start** transitions instantly, and **step-end** waits the full duration and then transitions instantly. The **step-start** value appears the same as if no transition was applied, and **step-end** appears as though a delay was set before another instant change. To be honest, it's difficult to see when you would want to use either of these.

Cubic Bézier Curves

If you've ever worked with the pen tool in any graphics program, then you've worked with Bézier curves to model smooth curves that can be mathematically reproduced at any scale.

In animation, you use Bézier curves to smooth time changes, most commonly at the start and end of the animation.

You define a cubic Bézier curve with four control points, P0, P1, P2, P3, which you can see in **FIGURE 3.4**. Point P0 is always 0,0 and point P3 is always 1,1. You use timing functions to define points P1 and P2.

FIGURE 3.4
Cubic Bézier curve

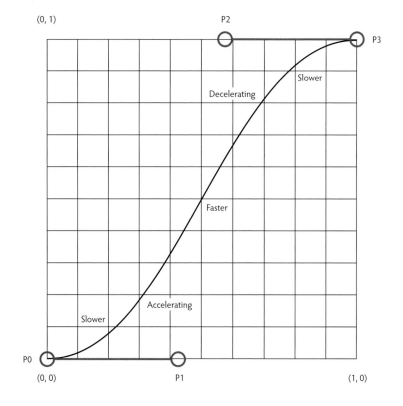

The curve usually does not pass through either P1 or P2. The points provide direction information but don't have to be on the curve itself. The curve is determined by mathematical formulas for each of the x and y values of the different points P0–P3. Here are the formulas for the x and y values:

```
x[t] = x0 + 3t(x1 - x2) + 3t^2(x0 + x1 - 2x1) +
⟶ t^3(x3 - x0 + 3x1 - 3x2)

y[t] = y0 + 3t(y1 - y2) + 3t^2(y0 + y1 - 2y1) +
⟶ t^3(y3 - y0 + 3y1 - 3y2)
```

You don't need to know the math to work with Bézier curves. You need only to define the points in the function. The more horizontal the segment of the curve, the slower the movement, and consequently, the more vertical the curve the faster the movement (Figure 3.4).

The function takes four numbers, and you might think it's one for each of the four different points P0–P3, but you're actually defining the x and y values for points P1 and P2. Both x values (the first and third numbers) must be between 0 and 1 or the definition is invalid.

```
transition-timing-function: cubic-bezier(<number>,
⟶ <number>, <number>, <number>)
```

There are keywords for the more common curves, so you don't have to set the actual points. The same way the transform functions maps to specific transform matrices, the keyword values for the timing function maps to specific Bézier curves.

Remember, the more horizontal the curve, the slower, and the more vertical, the faster. Curves that change from horizontal to vertical are accelerating, and curves that change from vertical to horizontal are decelerating.

Let's take a look at each of the curves for the keyword values (Figures 3.5 through 3.9).

- **ease**—Equivalent to **cubic-bezier(0.25, 0.1, 0.25, 1.0)**. At the beginning, the curve gets more vertical and accelerates before flattening out and getting much slower at the end (**FIGURE 3.5**). It gets its name because it eases into the curve by not accelerating too much.

FIGURE 3.5
Ease curve

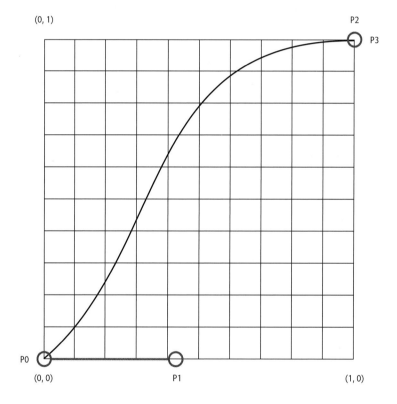

◆ `linear`—Equivalent to `cubic-bezier(0.0, 0.0, 1.0, 1.0)`. In a linear
cubic Bézier , curve points P0 and P1 have the same values as do points P2
and P3 (**FIGURE 3.6**). This effectively leaves two points, and the curve moves
linearly between them. In other words, the speed is constant from start to
end and there's no acceleration or deceleration at any point along the curve.

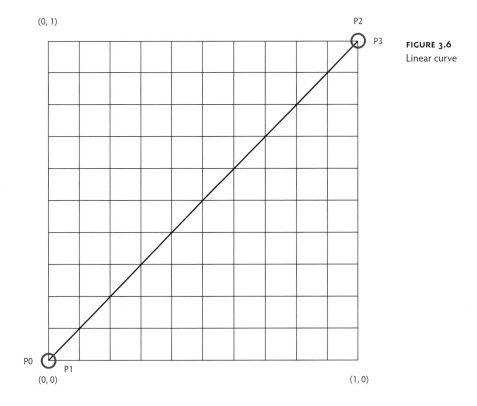

(0, 1)

P2

P3

FIGURE 3.6
Linear curve

P0

P1

(0, 0)

(1, 0)

◆ **ease-in**—Equivalent to **cubic-bezier(0.42, 0, 1.0, 1.0)**. This curve accelerates at the start until it reaches a more consistent speed (**FIGURE 3.7**). Points P2 and P3 are equal.

FIGURE 3.7
Ease-in curve

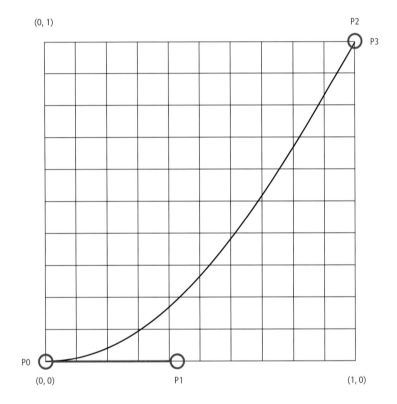

◆ **ease-out**—Equivalent to `cubic-bezier(0, 0, 0.58, 1.0)`. It is the opposite of **ease-in**. Speed is consistent at the start with P0 and P1 being the same (**FIGURE 3.8**). The curve decelerates toward the end.

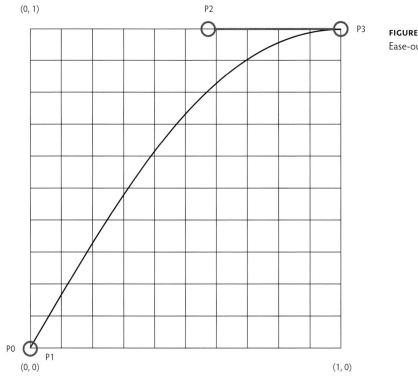

(0, 1)   P2   P3   **FIGURE 3.8**
                                        Ease-out curve

P0

P1

(0, 0)   (1, 0)

◆ `ease-in-out`—Equivalent to `cubic-bezier(0.42, 0, 0.58, 1.0)`. This curve is a combination of `ease-in` and `ease-out`. The curve accelerates at the start and decelerates at the end (**FIGURE 3.9**). The curve is symmetrical. The start of the curve accelerates by the same amount that it decelerates at the end.

FIGURE 3.9
Ease-in-out curve

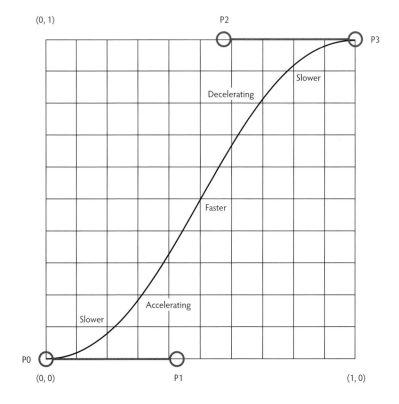

Lea Verou created a tool (cubic-bezier.com) that you can use to play around with different Bézier curves and compare the ones you create with the keyword curves described here. It's a great way to get a feel for the effect of each type of curve.

transition-delay Property

Until now, any transition you've started began the moment you triggered it. Hover over an element with a transition set and the transition begins the moment your mouse enters into the bounding box of the element.

The `transition-delay` property allows you to delay the start of the transition so it begins at some time after the transition is triggered.

```
transition-delay: 1.5s
```

By default, the value is `0s`, which means the transition executes immediately. Positive values delay the transition. Negative values are valid, which might surprise you. When the delay is set to a negative value, the transition happens instantly, but it appears as though it began at some point in the past. In other words, it begins partway through the transition.

Let's rework the example from early in this section when we stepped through several color changes. This example uses a stepped `timing-function` because it makes this particular point easier to see (**EXAMPLE 3.6**).

1. Create a new HTML document, and add the following HTML:

   ```
   <div class="box"></div>
   ```

2. Give the box dimensions, an initial `background-color`, and a different color on hover. The following code uses the same blue and red from earlier:

   ```
   .box {
       width: 200px;
       height: 200px;
       background-color: #33f;
   }

   .box:hover {
       background-color: #f33;
   }
   ```

3. Set the different `transition-*` properties on the `.box` class. Add [...] the code are highlighted.

```
.box {
    width: 200px;
    height: 200px;
    background-color: #33f;


    -webkit-transition-property: background-color;
        transition-property: background-color;

    -webkit-transition-duration: 5s;
        transition-duration: 5s;

    -webkit-transition-timing-function: steps(5, start);
        transition-timing-function: steps(5, start);

    -webkit-transition-delay: 2s;
        transition-delay: 2s;
}
```

NOTE

The code in Example 3.6 creates two boxes: one for the 2-second transition delay and one for the negative 2-second delay. This way you can easily see both at the same time. The code for this example won't match exactly the code in the file.

The last lines of this CSS are new with a 2-second delay.

4. Run the example in a browser.

Two seconds pass, and then the transition begins to change through each of the five distinct steps. Note that the change occurs at the end of the step, so from 0 to 2 seconds, nothing happens. Then a second passes, and a change occurs, and so on until the end.

5. Change the `transition-delay` to `-2s`, while leaving everything else the same.

```
transition-delay: -2s;
```

6. Run the new code in a browser, and observe the difference (**FIGURE 3.10**).

The transition begins instantly, but it skips the first two steps. It also appears to last 3 seconds as opposed to 5 seconds. The first 2 seconds and first two step intervals appear to occur prior to the transition starting.

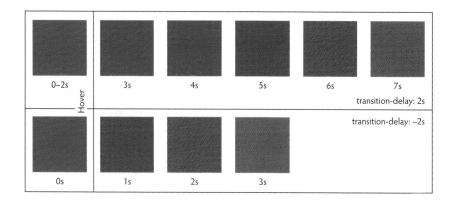

FIGURE 3.10
transition-delay

transition shorthand Property

As you saw earlier in this chapter, you can use the shorthand **transition** property instead of each individual property. Initial values are the initial values for each of the individual **transition-*** properties. In practice, you'll likely use the shorthand more than the individual properties.

```
transition: [ none | <single-transition-property> ] ||
 → <time> || <single-transition-timing-function> || <time>
```

Order is important: property, duration, timing function, and delay. The first time value is the duration, and the second time value is the delay.

Note that if there is more than one **transition-property** and the value of any of them is **none**, the entire declaration is invalid.

You can add multiple transitions using the shorthand method, but be careful with your commas. They go only between each new set of transitions.

```
.box {
    transition: background-color 2s ease-in 0.5s,
     → width 3s ease-out 0.25s;
}
```

Starting and Reversing Transitions

In Example 3.1, I showed how a transition could be applied on either side of the change. You first added the transition directly to the `.box div` and later switched so the transition was on the `:hover` state of the `.box` instead. The results were the same.

If you've been following along and typing the examples in this chapter, you've likely noticed that the transition reverses itself when you move your cursor outside the `.box div`. In the examples, the `.box` transitions from blue to red on hover, and then reverses itself back from red to blue over the same duration, delay, and timing function when you remove the hover.

You can not only set the transition on either state, you can set different `transition-*` properties for either the forward or reverse transition. Take a look at the following code:

```css
.box {
    -webkit-transition: background-color 2s ease-in;
            transition: background-color 2s ease-in;
}

.box:hover {
    -webkit-transition: background-color 5s ease-out;
            transition: background-color 5s ease-out;
}
```

This code sets similar transitions on both the initial and hover states of the `.box div`. In both cases, the code transitions the `background-color`. The `transition-duration` is `2s` and `5s` respectively, and the `transition-timing-function`s are `ease-in` and `ease-out`. The `transition-delay` isn't specified on either, so it's the default of `0s`.

What do you think will happen? Will the transition last 2 seconds or 5 seconds? Will it `ease-in` or `ease-out`? Will both transitions apply, and if so which applies on hover and which applies when the hover is removed?

The values set on each state control the transition to that state. In other words, both transitions apply. When you hover over the `.box div`, the transition set on the `:hover` state takes effect. In this example, that means when you hover over the element, the transition occurs over a 5-second duration, and it eases out.

When removing the hover and returning to the initial state, the values set on the initial `.box` class take effect. The transition takes only 2 seconds to return, and its timing function is `ease-in`.

Transitions can be interrupted. A good example is the `:hover` state for triggering the transitions. If a color change takes 5 seconds to complete, there's a good chance the user will have removed the cursor and stopped hovering before those 5 seconds are up.

If the reverse transition takes effect when the forward one is interrupted, it can be jarring. The forward transition has not completed, and its value will be one of the intermediate values. The reverse transition wants to start at what would have been the final value and then proceed through the entire duration of the transition.

The expectation from users is for the reverse transition to start where the forward transition ends, and have its duration reduced to however long the forward transition lasted before the interruption. Users expect to see the forward transition in reverse and not the reverse transition.

Fortunately, the rules are adjusted to meet the expectation.

* The end value of the interrupted `transition-property` becomes the start value for the reverse `transition-property`.

* A reverse shortening factor is computed.

* The reverse shortening factor is used to adjust the `transition-duration` of the reverse transition.

* The reverse shortening factor is used to adjust the `transition-delay` of the reverse transition if it's negative.

Transition Events

When a transition completes, it generates a DOM event. The Document Object Model (DOM) is an application programming interface (API) for valid HTML. It allows for communication between JavaScript and HTML, which is how you'll use it here.

Each property that completes its transition fires an event. Because of this, you can time other actions to sync with the completion of a transition.

It's important to note that this event is fired only when the transition completes. The event doesn't fire if the transition is interrupted.

Assuming completion, the event that gets fired can be accessed as `transitionend` (transition end without the space). In Webkit, it's `webkitTransitionEnd`, and in Opera it's `oTransitionEnd`. Note the difference in camel case between the vendor-prefixed events and the non-vendor-prefixed event.

The `transitionend` event offers three read-only values you can access:

- `PropertyName`—A string indicating the name of the property that completed its transition.

- `ElapsedTime`—A float indicating the number of seconds the transition had been running at the time the `transitionend` event fired. This value isn't affected by the value of `transition-delay`.

- `PseudoElement`—A string with the name of the pseudo-element on which the transition occurred. An empty string is returned when the transition wasn't applied to a pseudo-element.

You can listen for the event with the following JavaScript:

```
el.addEventListener("transitionend", updateTransition,
→ true);
```

`updateTransition` is a function call, which includes code for what should happen when the event completes. It can be named anything you want as long as the function call matches the name of the function. How about an example (**EXAMPLE 3.7**)?

1. Create a new document, and add the following HTML. Create two boxes in your HTML, and give them both a **class** of **box**. Then give each a unique **id**. The following code uses the not-so-creative **one** and **two** as **id**s. Wrap both in a **.container div**, which you'll use to center things horizontally on the screen.

```
<div class="container">

    <div class="box" id="one"></div>

    <div class="box" id="two"></div>

</div>
```

2. Both boxes should look the same initially, so give the **.box class** some dimensions and a **background-color**. Add some margin to the bottom so the two boxes aren't directly touching each other. Don't forget to center the **.container div**.

```
.container{

    width: 200px;

    margin: 5em auto;

}

.box {

    margin: 0 0 5em 0;

    width: 200px;

    height: 200px;

    background-color: #33f;

}
```

At this point, you should see two identical boxes, one below the other.

3. Add a change in color to the **:hover** state of the first box with **id="one"** applied.

```
#one:hover {

    background-color: #f33;

}
```

4. Then add a transition to the initial state of `.box #one`.

```css
#one {
    -webkit-transition: background-color 2s ease-in-out;
            transition: background-color 2s ease-in-out;
}
```

5. Run the code in a browser.

   The box on top transitions its **background-color** on hover, and the box below does nothing. This is all familiar by now. Time for something new. Time for some JavaScript.

6. Add the following JavaScript to your document in between **<script> </script>** tags:

```html
<script>
var init = function() {
    var box = document.getElementById("one");
    var box2 = document.getElementById("two");

    box.addEventListener("webkitTransitionEnd",
     → updateTransition, false);
    box.addEventListener("oTransitionEnd",
     → updateTransition, false);
    box.addEventListener("transitionend",
     → updateTransition, false);

    function updateTransition () {
        box2.style.backgroundColor = "#f33";
    }
};

window.addEventListener('DOMContentLoaded', init, false);
</script>
```

7. Reload your page in a browser.

When you hover over `.box #one`, it transitions from blue to red.

Don't remove your cursor, and let the transition complete the change in color to red. The moment it does, the `background-color` of `.box #two` also changes to red, although it does so instantly (**FIGURE 3.11**).

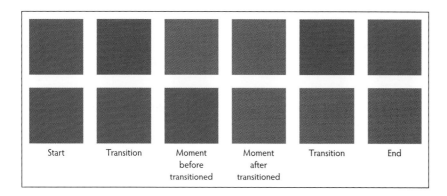

FIGURE 3.11
Transition events

Start   Transition   Moment before transitioned   Moment after transitioned   Transition   End

Once `.box #two` has changed `background-color`, remove your cursor to release the hover. Notice that `.box #one` reverses its transition, but `.box #two` doesn't. You changed the `background-color` of `.box #two` through JavaScript, but you did nothing to change it back to its initial `background-color`.

Here's what is happing, starting with the last line of the JavaScript, `window.addEventListener('DOMContentLoaded', init, false);`. This is telling the browser to wait until the DOM is loaded and when it is to run the `init` function. Everything above this line of code is the `init` function.

The `init` function first finds the two elements (the `.box`es) by their `id`s and assigns each to a different variable (`box` and `box2`). The function next adds an event listener (along with vendor-prefixed versions) to box (`.box #one`). When the transition event is fired, the function `updateTransition` is set to run.

Finally, `updateTransition` changes the `background-color` of box2 (`.box #two`) to red (`#f33`).

You can make more changes in `updateTransition` if you'd like.

8. Change the `updateTransition` function so it looks like the following. Additions to the code are highlighted (**EXAMPLE 3.8**).

```
function updateTransition () {
    box.style.width = 500 + "px";
    box2.style.backgroundColor = "#f33";
}
```

Instead of changing only the color of box2 (`.box #two`), you're now also changing the width of box (`.box #one`).

9. Reload your page with the new function. Hover over `.box #one`, and when the transition ends, `.box #one` will get wider at the same time `.box #two` changes `background-color` (**FIGURE 3.12**). Both changes occur instantly.

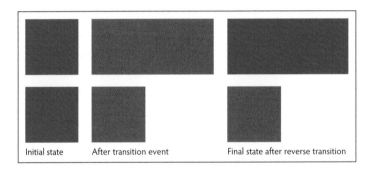

Initial state   After transition event   Final state after reverse transition

This is a rather simple example, but hopefully your imagination is kicking in with ideas for other things you can chain to the completion of a transition event.

Animatable Properties

Something you might have wondered while reading through this chapter is what can be transitioned. The examples used `background-color` to keep things simple, but you certainly aren't limited to transitioning the `background-color` of various elements.

Unfortunately, you can't transition every CSS property. Not every CSS property is animatable, and not every browser has implemented the necessary code to make all animatable properties able to be transitioned.

The W3C spec provides a list of CSS 2.1 properties that are animatable as well as which CSS3 color module properties are animatable. In addition, newer properties, such as the `flexbox order` property (www.w3.org/TR/css3-flexbox/#order-property), now lists whether or not they're animatable (**FIGURE 3.13**).

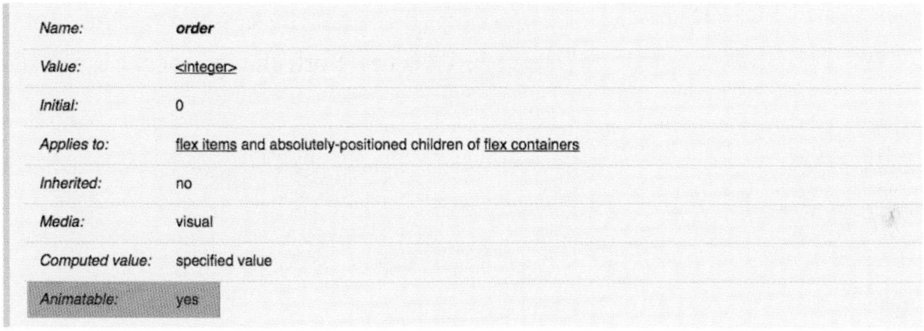

Name:	*order*
Value:	<u><integer></u>
Initial:	0
Applies to:	<u>flex items</u> and absolutely-positioned children of <u>flex containers</u>
Inherited:	no
Media:	visual
Computed value:	specified value
Animatable:	yes

FIGURE 3.13
The `flexbox order` property is animatable.

In addition to the property itself, you have to consider the value type of the property. For example, margins and paddings can have values that are a length in px or as a percentage; however, only the length value is animatable according to the spec.

Then again some browsers have implemented support for transitioning percentages on margins and paddings while they haven't implemented the same support on percentages for a property like `word-spacing`, which the spec says should have support.

The point is that any list of animatable properties and value types is going to be somewhat fluid. **TABLE 3.1** lists the property names and value types from the CSS3 Transitions spec. This list may have changed between the time of this writing and the time you're reading this book. In the next section are a few webpages that show similar tables.

TABLE 3.1 CSS3 TRANSITIONS PROPERTY NAMES AND VALUE TYPES

PROPERTY	TYPE
`background-color`	color
`background-position`	repeatable list of simple list of length, percentage, or calc
`border-bottom-color`	color
`border-bottom-width`	length
`border-left-color`	color
`border-left-width`	length
`border-right-color`	color
`border-right-width`	length
`border-spacing`	simple list of length
`border-top-color`	color
`border-top-width`	length
`bottom`	length, percentage, or calc
`clip`	rectangle
`color`	color
`font-size`	length
`font-weight`	font weight
`height`	length, percentage, or calc
`left`	length, percentage, or calc
`letter-spacing`	length
`line-height`	either number or length
`margin-bottom`	length
`margin-left`	length
`margin-right`	length
`margin-top`	length
`max-height`	length, percentage, or calc
`max-width`	length, percentage, or calc
`min-height`	length, percentage, or calc

TABLE 3.1   (CONTINUED)

PROPERTY	TYPE
min-width	length, percentage, or calc
opacity	number
outline-color	color
outline-width	length
padding-bottom	length
padding-left	length
padding-right	length
padding-top	length
right	length, percentage, or calc
text-indent	length, percentage, or calc
text-shadow	shadow list
top	length, percentage, or calc
vertical-align	length
visibility	visibility
width	length, percentage, or calc
word-spacing	length
z-index	integer

Animatable Property List Resources

The following webpages contain frequently updated lists of animatable properties:

- www.w3.org/TR/css3-transitions/#animatable-properties

- www.opera.com/docs/specs/presto2.12/css/transitions

- http://oli.jp/2010/css-animatable-properties

- http://thewebevolved.com/support/animation/properties

- https://developer.mozilla.org/en-US/docs/Web/CSS/CSS_animated_properties

Summary

Transitions are one way to add a time frame to website element changes. They're simple animations between a beginning state and an ending state, and they must be triggered in some way to take effect.

Browser support is not only good, it's better than it was for the transforms you saw in the previous chapter.

You can set values on a handful of **transition-*** properties or you can use the transition shorthand:

◆ `transition-property`

◆ `transition-duration`

◆ `transition-timing-function`

◆ `transition-delay`

◆ `transition`

You can add multiple transitions to a single element, and you can add different transitions on different states of the same element. When you do the latter, the transition on the state being transitioned to is the one that browsers use.

Each time a transition completes, it fires an event that you can hook in to via JavaScript to time another change with the completed transition. One way to use this ability is to chain transitions one after another to have more than a single beginning and end.

Another way to do the same is to use CSS keyframe animation, which brings us to the subject of the next chapter.

CHAPTER 4

ANIMATIONS

CSS transitions offer you a way to create simple animations that always start as the result of triggering a CSS property change. Transitions can animate only between a start and end state, and each state is controlled by existing CSS property values. For example, a transition that runs on hover transitions between values on the element and values on the hover state of the element. Overall, transitions are a simple way to animate but offer little control over the animation.

CSS animations provide a bit more control. They allow for the creation of multiple keyframes (**FIGURE 4.1**) over which the animation occurs. While they can start in reaction to a change in CSS property value, they can also run on their own. An animation executes as soon as the `animation` property is applied.

FIGURE 4.1
Animation keyframes

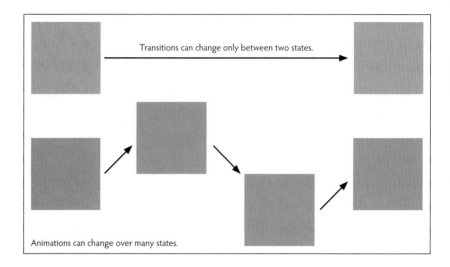

Transitions don't change property values; they define how the change occurs. Animations can change property values inside each keyframe.

Transitions change implicitly. You define things at the start and end states, and you leave it to the browser to determine all the intermediate states. Animations change explicitly. The animation can define start and end states as well as some intermediate states. The browser still determines the intermediate states between keyframes, but the animation gets to define as many keyframes as it wants.

All the things you could change when working with transitions, you can still change when working with animations. You determine how long the animation lasts and what `timing-function` to use between keyframes. You also get to delay the animation if you like.

In addition, you can decide how many times the animation should run and in which direction it should run. You can set the animation to be running or paused. You can even determine which CSS property values apply outside the time frame in which the animation runs.

Animations have other benefits over transitions as you'll see in this chapter. In general, these benefits are about giving you more control. Transitions have advantages over CSS animations, too. In general, they're about the simplicity of transitions.

Browser Support

Browser support for CSS animations is good. It's similar to what you saw earlier for transforms and transitions. CSS animations work in all modern browsers. In IE10 and newer, Firefox, and IE Mobile, no vendor prefixes are needed.

Safari, Chrome, Opera, iOS Safari, Android Browser, and Blackberry Browser all use the `-webkit` vendor prefix, so you have only the one prefix to deal with. The `animation-fill-mode` property isn't supported in Android below version 2.3. In iOS 6.1 and earlier, animations aren't supported on `pseudo-element`s.

As you probably expect by this point, the holdouts are Opera Mini and IE9 and earlier. Unfortunately, there's no polyfill like there was for transforms and transitions. The fallback is to create the animation using JavaScript: You first check to detect CSS animation support and then use one of the available JavaScript libraries for working with animation.

JavaScript animation is beyond the scope of this book, but the following section gives you to a few places where you can find more information.

Detecting Browser Support

Here are some resources for detecting support as well as some JavaScript animation libraries:

- https://hacks.mozilla.org/2011/09/detecting-and-generating-css-animations-in-javascript

- https://developer.mozilla.org/en-US/docs/Web/Guide/CSS/Using_CSS_animations/Detecting_CSS_animation_support

Finding JavaScript Libraries for Animation

The most popular library is—without doubt—jQuery, although it's not the most performant way to create animations with JavaScript. Here are some other options:

- http://api.jquery.com/animate

- www.polymer-project.org/platform/web-animations.html

- https://github.com/web-animations/web-animations-js

- http://updates.html5rocks.com/2014/05/Web-Animations---element-animate-is-now-in-Chrome-36

You could create animations for every browser using JavaScript and ignore CSS animations completely. If you're using JavaScript to create the animation for some browsers, why not use JavaScript for all browsers and not worry so much about CSS animation support? CSS animations are usually, though not always, more performant than the same animation in JavaScript.

Another option, and the one I recommend, is to treat CSS animations as part of the noncritical experience. Use animations to enhance the design and the design's aesthetic, but make sure nothing breaks in browsers that don't support CSS animations. Your site should still work in any browser that doesn't support animations, but it can provide a more enjoyable experience for those that can.

Note that while CSS animations work in modern browsers, you don't necessarily see the same smoothness. A smooth-running animation in one browser might look a bit jerky in another, and it's not always the same browsers looking smooth or not. It depends on the browser and the specifics of the animation.

CSS Animations

As we've been doing throughout this book, let's start with an example.

CSS Positioning

You'll make a box slide across the screen from left to right in two ways. The first way will be to use CSS positioning (**EXAMPLE 4.1**).

1. Add a `div` with a class of `box` to your HTML.

   ```
   <div class="box"></div>
   ```

2. Give the `.box div` dimensions and a background color so you can see it on the page. Set its `position` to `absolute`. Top and left values will be 0 by default, which is fine for this example.

   ```
   .box {
       width: 200px;
       height: 200px;
       background-color: #393;
       position: absolute;
   }
   ```

You need two components to create the animation. The first one declares the animation on `.box`. Part of the benefit of the `animation` property is the name of a keyframe where you'll change properties, so you also need to create this keyframe, which is the second component.

3. Add the `animation` property to `.box`.

```
.box {
    -webkit-animation: slide 5s linear 0s 3;
            animation: slide 5s linear 0s 3;
}
```

The first value in the list is `slide`, which is the name of your keyframe.

4. Create the `slide` keyframe.

```
@-webkit-keyframes slide {

    from {
        left:0
    }

    to {
        left: 600px
    }

}

@keyframes slide {

    from {
        left: 0;
    }

    to {
        left: 600px;
    }

}
```

5. Load the file in a browser.

A green square appears in the upper-left corner of your browser. As soon as the page loads, it moves 600 pixels to the right, jumps back to the upper-left corner, slides to the right again, and repeats a third time before finally returning to the upper-left corner and stopping (**FIGURE 4.2**).

FIGURE 4.2
Slide animation using the
`left` property

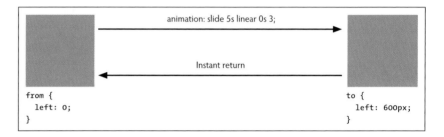

The animation itself probably wasn't very smooth, but you'll get to that in a moment. Let's talk about what the code is doing, starting with the keyframe.

The keyframe has the name `slide`. It includes two declarations for the `left` property, once in a `from` state and once in a `to` state. In the `from` state, the `left` value is `0`, and in the `to` state, the value is `600px`. The states `from` and `to` represent the start and end states, so initially the `.box` is positioned 0 pixels from the left edge, and at the end of the animation cycle, it is 600 pixels from the left edge.

To start the animation, you set the animation shorthand property on the `.box div`.

```
animation: slide 5s linear 0s 3;
```

The animation is calling the keyframe named `slide`, and it runs for a duration of 5 seconds. The `timing-function` is linear. There's no delay, and the animation is set to run three times.

Smoothing the Animation

What about the jumpiness in the animation? Let's modify the example to move the `.box` with a transform instead of changing the value of the `left` property (**EXAMPLE 4.2**). You need to adjust only the keyframe.

1. Replace the keyframe in step 4 of Example 4.1 with the following keyframe:

```
@-webkit-keyframes slide {

    to {
        -webkit-transform: translate(600px, 0px);
          -ms-transform: translate(600px, 0px);
              transform: translate(600px, 0px);
    }

}

@keyframes slide {

    to {
        -webkit-transform: translate(600px, 0px);
          -ms-transform: translate(600px, 0px);
              transform: translate(600px, 0px);
    }

}
```

   In this code, the `translate` function moves the `.box div` 600 pixels to the right, the same as the `left` values did in the previous `@keyframes` rule. Notice that only the `to` state is included this time. You don't need to include a `from` state. You really didn't need it the first time either. The initial state of the `.box div` as set on the `.box` class is exactly what you want for the `from` state, so there isn't a need to explicitly set it in the keyframe.

2. Reload your page with this new keyframe.

   The same thing happens as before: A green `.box` moves 600 pixels to the right three times (**FIGURE 4.3**). However, this time the animation runs smoother. We'll get to why at the end of the chapter. For now just know there are multiple ways to create an animation (or a transition), but the performance of each way can vary.

FIGURE 4.3
Slide animation using
`translate` function

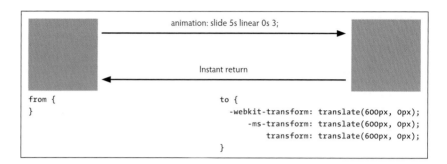

As you can see in the example, animations can reset CSS property values inside their keyframes. Transitions can't do this. Although CSS animations affect property values while running, they don't by default control values before the animation starts or after it ends. By default, the intrinsic styles (styles added directly to the element and not inside keyframes) of the element control the values outside the time the animation is running. The styles set in the keyframe are in control while the animation is running, but not necessarily before or after. You do have a measure of control to change the default.

It's possible to have multiple animations running at the same time and for each animation to set different values on the same property. When this happens, the animation defined last in the list of keyframe names overrides the other animations, and the value it sets is used.

Animations can start in one of two ways:

◆ On page load

◆ In reaction to a CSS property change

The start time of an animation is the latter of the time when the style specifying the animation changes (changing the element on hover for example) or the time the document's **load** event is fired—in other words, automatically after the page has loaded.

The @Keyframes Rule

Keyframes are the different states of the element being animated. They're used to specify different values for the properties being animated at various points during the animation. A series of keyframes defines the behavior for one cycle through the animation. Remember animations can repeat multiple times.

You define keyframes inside the `@keyframes` rule.

```
@keyframes identifier {
    List of properties and values
}
```

An `@keyframes` rule begins with the `@keyframes` keyword followed by an identifier (the keyframe name). Inside the brackets is a list of CSS properties and values to set the style for the specific states.

Inside each `@keyframes` rule is a list of percent values or the keywords **to** and **from**. The keyword **from** is equivalent to **0%**, and the keyword **to** is equivalent to **100%**. When using a percent, the % sign needs to be included. **0** and **100** are invalid values; **0%** and **100%** are the correct values.

```
@Keyframes slide {

    0% {
            left: 0;
    }

    20% {
            left: 100px;
    }

    40% {
            left: 200px;
    }
```

```
60% {

        left: 300px;

}


80% {

        left: 400px;

}


100% {

        left: 500px;

}


}
```

This @keyframes rule could also be written as

```
@Keyframes slide {

    from {

        left: 0;

    }


    20% {

        left: 100px;

    }


    40% {

        left: 200px;

    }


    60% {

        left: 300px;

    }
```

```
    80% {

         left: 400px;

    }


    to {

         left: 500px;

    }


}
```

Each keyframe selector specifies the percentage of the animation's duration that the specific keyframe represents. The keyframe state is specified by the group of properties and values declared on the selector.

If you don't set a keyframe at `0%` (or `from`), then the browser constructs a `0%` state using the intrinsic values of the properties being animated. Similarly if no `100%` (or `to`) keyframe is set, the browser constructs the state from intrinsic values. Negative percent values or values greater than 100% are ignored. Keyframes containing properties that aren't animatable or contain invalid properties are ignored.

`@keyframes` rules don't cascade. A single animation will never use keyframes from more than one `@keyframes` rule. When multiple `@keyframes` have been specified on the `animation-name` property, the last one in the list (ordered by time) with a matching `@keyframes` rule controls the animation.

It's valid for an `@keyframes` rule to be empty, and because of this it can be used to hide keyframes previously defined. The empty `@keyframes` rule should come later in your CSS to override any `@keyframes` rule with the same identifier that appears earlier in your CSS.

1. Add the following after the `@keyframes` rules you set in Example 4.1.

    ```
    @-webkit-keyframes slide {

    }


    @keyframes slide {

    }
    ```

NOTE

I'm using the words "keyframe" and "keyframes" in ways that might be confusing. Each percentage value represents a new keyframe or state with its own CSS property values. Together the properties and values in each keyframe make up a keyframe declaration block. The `@keyframes` rule is the special @ rule that contains all the different keyframes (states) that an animation runs through.

2. Reload your webpage. The animation should no longer run, since an empty `@keyframes` rule is called.

3. Remove the empty `@keyframes` rule or place it before the nonempty `@keyframes` rule, and the animation will run again.

animation-* Properties

CSS animations offer eight different properties for controlling an animation. Some are comparable to similarly named `transition-*` properties, and some will be new.

animation-name Property

The `animation-name` property defines a comma-separated list of animations to apply to the given selector. It's similar to the `transition-property` in that it ultimately defines the properties that are animated. With the `transition-property`, those properties are explicitly named. With the `animation-name`, an `@keyframes` rule is explicitly named, and that rule contains the properties that will be animated.

```
-webkit-animation-name: slide, drop;
        animation-name: slide, drop;
```

Each `animation-name` in the list should match a specific `@keyframes` rule.

```
@-webkit-keyframes slide {
    properties: values;
}


@keyframes slide {
    properties: values;
}
```

```
@-webkit-keyframes drop {
    properties: values;
}

@keyframes drop {
    properties: values;
}
```

If there's no match in keyframe name (identifier), the animation won't run. In addition to the identifier of an `@keyframes` rule, a value of **none** is also valid. When the **none** keyword value is used, no animation runs. You can use **none** to override an animation that's inherited from a parent element.

```
-webkit-animation-name: none;
        animation-name: none;
```

`@keyframes` change the value of CSS properties. If multiple animations try to change the value of the same property on an element, the animation closest to the last name in the `animation-name` list controls the property values.

If multiple `animation-name`s are listed and one is removed, it stops running, but the other listed animations continue.

Every listed `animation-name` should have a corresponding value for any other `animation-*` properties. If there are too many values in an `animation-*` property, any leftover values are ignored. If there aren't enough values, the list of values will be repeated until there are enough to match.

Animations are applied to elements with an `animation-name` value that matches the name of an `@keyframes` rule. Once applied, the animation runs. It runs once the page loads unless it's been applied to a trigger, such as `:hover`. Once started, an animation continues to run until it finishes or the `animation-name` value is removed, such as removing the `:hover` on the animating element.

An animation ends based on some combination of the `animation-duration`, `animation-iteration-count`, and `animation-fill` mode properties. You can also end an animation by setting the animated element's `display` property to **none**. This also ends any animations running on descendant elements.

NOTE

When an **animation-name** is added to the **:hover** state of an element, removing the hover also removes the **animation-name**, and the animation stops.

Changing the value of an animation element's **display** property to something other than **none** immediately starts that animation. It also starts any animations applied to descendants of the parent element. Changing the value of **display** is one more way you can turn on and off an animation.

The values in each keyframe in an **@keyframes** rule are held as a snapshot when the animation starts. Changing the intrinsic property on an element with an animation running has no effect. The values in the animation are in control until the animation stops.

animation-duration Property

The **animation-duration** property defines how long an animation lasts during one cycle of the animation. It's similar to the **transition-duration** property and takes a time value in seconds (s) or milliseconds (ms).

```
-webkit-animation-duration: 10s;

    animation-duration: 10s;
```

Like **transition-duration**, the default value is **0s**, which is why elements don't animate automatically even when they're animatable. Technically, they are animating, but everything happens in an instant.

Note that **animation-duration** is the length of one full cycle of the animation. It's not the length of each keyframe in the **@keyframes** rule. For example, if you set an **animation-duration** of **10s** and have the following **@keyframes** rule

```
@Keyframes duration {

    0% {

        property: value;

    }

    50% {

        property: value;

    }
```

```
100% {

      property: value;

   }
}
```

the animation will take 10 seconds to get from 0 percent to 100 percent, and not 10 seconds to go from 0 percent to 50 percent and then 10 seconds more from 50 percent to 100 percent.

Similarly, when an animation is set to loop multiple times, the `animation-duration` is the time it takes to complete one loop or cycle.

animation-timing-function Property

The `animation-timing-function` property describes an acceleration curve for each keyframe in a single animation cycle. It's similar to the `transition-timing-function`. You can use any of the keyword timing functions or create one of your own.

```
animation-timing-function: step-start;
animation-timing-function: step-end;
animation-timing-function: steps();
animation-timing-function: ease;
animation-timing-function: linear;
animation-timing-function: ease-in;
animation-timing-function: ease-out;
animation-timing-function: ease-in-out;
animation-timing-function: cubic-bezier();
```

Note that the `animation-timing-function` applies between keyframes and not over the entire animation cycle. This means if you have keyframes at `0%`, `50%`, and `100%` and an `animation-timing-function` of `ease-in`, the animation eases into each of the three keyframes in the `@keyframes` rule and not just once at the beginning of the animation.

Let's try an example to see this more clearly (**EXAMPLE 4.3**).

1. Add a `div` with a class of `box` to your HTML.

   ```html
   <div class="box"></div>
   ```

2. Give the `.box` class dimensions and a `background-color`.

   ```css
   .box {
       width: 200px;
       height: 200px;
       background-color: #393;
   }
   ```

3. Add an animation to the `.box div` using the individual `animation-*` properties.

   ```css
   .box {
       -webkit-animation-name: slide;
               animation-name: slide;

       -webkit-animation-duration: 5s;
               animation-duration: 5s;

       -webkit-animation-timing-function: ease-in;
               animation-timing-function: ease-in;
   }
   ```

4. Finally add an `@keyframes` rule to your CSS.

   ```css
   @-webkit-keyframes slide {

       0% {
           -webkit-transform: translate(0px, 0px);
              -ms-transform: translate(0px, 0px);
                  transform: translate(0px, 0px);
       }
   ```

```
    25% {
        -webkit-transform: translate(150px, 0px);
            -ms-transform: translate(150px, 0px);
                transform: translate(150px, 0px);
    }

    50% {
        -webkit-transform: translate(300px, 0px);
            -ms-transform: translate(300px, 0px);
                transform: translate(300px, 0px);
    }

    75% {
        -webkit-transform: translate(450px, 0px);
            -ms-transform: translate(450px, 0px);
                transform: translate(450px, 0px);
    }

    100% {
        -webkit-transform: translate(600px, 0px);
            -ms-transform: translate(600px, 0px);
                transform: translate(600px, 0px);
    }

}

@keyframes slide {

    0% {
        -webkit-transform: translate(0px, 0px);
            -ms-transform: translate(0px, 0px);
```

```
            transform: translate(0px, 0px);

    }

    25% {

        -webkit-transform: translate(150px, 0px);
            -ms-transform: translate(150px, 0px);
                transform: translate(150px, 0px);

    }

    50% {

        -webkit-transform: translate(300px, 0px);
            -ms-transform: translate(300px, 0px);
                transform: translate(300px, 0px);

    }

    75% {

        -webkit-transform: translate(450px, 0px);
            -ms-transform: translate(450px, 0px);
                transform: translate(450px, 0px);

    }

    100% {

        -webkit-transform: translate(600px, 0px);
            -ms-transform: translate(600px, 0px);
                transform: translate(600px, 0px);

    }

}
```

This code adds five keyframes to the `@keyframes` rule. This should make it easier to see that the `ease-in` timing function is running between each keyframe and not once over the entire animation cycle.

5. Load your page in a browser, and observe the timing curve between keyframes (**FIGURE 4.4**).

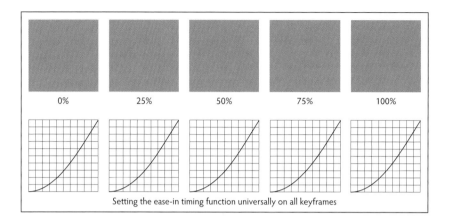

FIGURE 4.4
Animation timing functions

You can override the timing function inside each of the keyframes. When a timing function is applied inside a keyframe, it's instructing the animation to use that function moving from the keyframe with the timing function applied to the next one (**EXAMPLE 4.4**).

6. Replace your **@keyframes slide** rule from Example 4.3 with the following rule. Changes in the code are highlighted.

```
@-webkit-keyframes slide {

    0% {
        -webkit-transform: translate(0px, 0px);
            -ms-transform: translate(0px, 0px);
                transform: translate(0px, 0px);
    }

    25% {
        -webkit-transform: translate(150px, 0px);
            -ms-transform: translate(150px, 0px);
                transform: translate(150px, 0px);
```

```
            -webkit-animation-timing-function: linear;
                  animation-timing-function: linear;
    }

    50% {
        -webkit-transform: translate(300px, 0px);
            -ms-transform: translate(300px, 0px);
                transform: translate(300px, 0px);
    }

    75% {
        -webkit-transform: translate(450px, 0px);
            -ms-transform: translate(450px, 0px);
                transform: translate(450px, 0px);

        -webkit-animation-timing-function: linear;
              animation-timing-function: linear;
    }

    100% {
        -webkit-transform: translate(100px, 0px);
            -ms-transform: translate(100px, 0px);
                transform: translate(100px, 0px);
    }

}

@keyframes slide {

    0% {
        -webkit-transform: translate(0px, 0px);
            -ms-transform: translate(0px, 0px);
                transform: translate(0px, 0px);
    }
```

```
    25% {
        -webkit-transform: translate(150px, 0px);
          -ms-transform: translate(150px, 0px);
              transform: translate(150px, 0px);

        -webkit-animation-timing-function: linear;
                animation-timing-function: linear;
    }

    50% {
        -webkit-transform: translate(300px, 0px);
           -ms-transform: translate(300px, 0px);
               transform: translate(300px, 0px);
    }

    75% {
        -webkit-transform: translate(450px, 0px);
           -ms-transform: translate(450px, 0px);
               transform: translate(450px, 0px);

        -webkit-animation-timing-function: linear;
                animation-timing-function: linear;
    }

    100% {
        -webkit-transform: translate(100px, 0px);
           -ms-transform: translate(100px, 0px);
               transform: translate(100px, 0px);
    }

}
```

In this code, you override the `ease-in` timing function on two of the keyframes.

7. Reload your page, and observe the difference in the acceleration curve between keyframes (**FIGURE 4.5**).

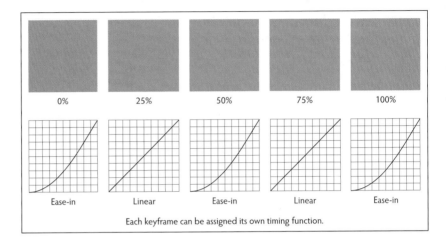

Each keyframe can be assigned its own timing function.

The way timing functions work over keyframes and the ability to override them on a specific keyframe is powerful and perhaps a bit scary. You have great control over how your animation accelerates, but you also have the responsibility to exercise that control. Having an animation ease in between every keyframe is probably not what you want.

animation-iteration-count Property

Transitions run once when triggered and run once in reverse when the trigger is removed. Animations can run as many times as you want. The `animation-iteration-count` property defines how many times an animation runs, and it takes as a value any number or the keyword `infinite`. The latter sets your animation to run in an endless loop.

```
-webkit-animation-iteration-count: 3;
        animation-iteration-count: 3;


-webkit-animation-iteration-count: infinite;
        animation-iteration-count: infinite;
```

You've already seen the `animation-iteration-count` in action in Example 4.1, although that example used the animation shorthand to set all the values. Because you might be getting tired of sliding boxes and because the rest of the examples in this chapter are variations of that same sliding box, let's do something different here (**EXAMPLE 4.5**).

1. Start by adding a `div` with a class of `box` to your HTML.

```
<div class="box"></div>
```

2. Instead of giving dimensions and a `background-color` to the `.box div`, set the dimensions to **0px**, and add a border with different colors for each side. Finally, give the border a radius of **50%**.

```
.box {
    width: 0px;
    height: 0px;
    border-width: 100px;
    border-style: solid;;
    border-color: #393 #933 #399 #993;
    border-radius: 50%;
}
```

3. Load your page.

A circle appears with four pie wedges, each a different color.

4. Add the following `animation-*` properties to `.box`. Note that you'll be rotating the `.box div` this time instead of moving it.

```
.box {
    -webkit-animation-name: rotate;
            animation-name: rotate;

    -webkit-animation-duration: 4s;
            animation-duration: 4s;

    -webkit-animation-timing-function: linear;
            animation-timing-function: linear;
```

```
        -webkit-animation-iteration-count: 3;
            animation-iteration-count: 3;
}
```

5. Create the rotate `@keyframes` rules to rotate the `.box` div.

```
@-webkit-keyframes rotate {

    0% {
        -webkit-transform: rotate(0deg);
          -ms-transform: rotate(0deg);
              transform: rotate(0deg);
    }

    25% {
        -webkit-transform: rotate(90deg);
          -ms-transform: rotate(90deg);
              transform: rotate(90deg);

    }

    50% {
        -webkit-transform: rotate(180deg);
          -ms-transform: rotate(180deg);
              transform: rotate(180deg);
    }

    75% {
        -webkit-transform: rotate(270deg);
          -ms-transform: rotate(270deg);
              transform: rotate(270deg);
    }
```

```
    100% {

        -webkit-transform: rotate(360deg);

            -ms-transform: rotate(360deg);

                transform: rotate(360deg);

    }

}

@keyframes rotate {

    0% {

        -webkit-transform: rotate(0deg);

            -ms-transform: rotate(0deg);

                transform: rotate(0deg);

    }

    25% {

        -webkit-transform: rotate(90deg);

            -ms-transform: rotate(90deg);

                transform: rotate(90deg);


    }

    50% {

        -webkit-transform: rotate(180deg);

            -ms-transform: rotate(180deg);

                transform: rotate(180deg);

    }
```

```
        75% {

                -webkit-transform: rotate(270deg);

                    -ms-transform: rotate(270deg);

                        transform: rotate(270deg);

        }


        100% {

                -webkit-transform: rotate(360deg);

                    -ms-transform: rotate(360deg);

                        transform: rotate(360deg);

        }


    }
```

6. Load your code in a browser.

The circular `.box div` rotates around its center.

If you followed the colors in the example for the borders, the green wedge should start at the top. Each time the green wedge is back at the top is one iteration or one animation cycle (**FIGURE 4.6**).

FIGURE 4.6
Animation iteration count

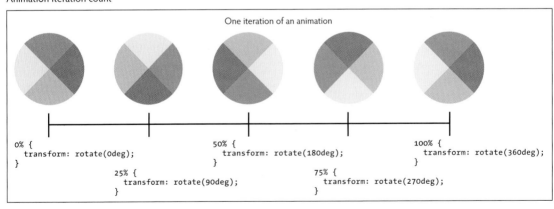

animation-direction Property

Another new property is the `animation-direction` property, which defines whether an animation runs forward or in reverse on some or all of its cycles. The `animation-direction` property takes one of four values:

- `normal` specifies that all iterations of the animation are played as specified.

- `reverse` specifies that all iterations of the animation are played in the reverse direction as specified.

- `alternate` causes the cycles to alternate between `normal` and `reverse` with `normal` for the first cycle and all odd iteration counts. Even counts are `reversed`.

- `alternate-reverse` causes the cycles to alternate between `normal` and `reverse` with `reverse` for the first cycle and all odd iteration counts. Even counts are `normal`.

```
-webkit-animation-direction: normal;
      animation-direction: normal;


-webkit-animation-direction: alternate-reverse;
      animation-direction: alternate-reverse;
```

When the animation plays in reverse, the timing functions also run in reverse—for example, `ease-in` runs as `ease-out`.

Until now, the sliding box you've been working with slides to the right and then instantly returns to its initial location. The jump is more than a little jarring. The `alternate` and `alternate-reverse` values can remove the jump. Instead, the box continues to slide right and left until the animation stops.

Let's go back to the sliding `.box div` you've used through most of this chapter (**EXAMPLE 4.6**).

1. Start by adding a `div` with a class of `box` to your HTML.

   ```
   <div class="box"></div>
   ```

2. Give the `.box div` dimensions and a background color.

```
.box {
    width: 200px;
    height: 200px;
    background-color: #393;
}
```

3. Add the `animation-*` properties to `.box`. Additions to the code are highlighted.

```
.box {
    -webkit-animation-name: slide;
            animation-name: slide;

    -webkit-animation-duration: 5s;
            animation-duration: 5s;

    -webkit-animation-timing-function: linear;
            animation-timing-function: linear;

    -webkit-animation-iteration-count: 3;
            animation-iteration-count: 3;

    -webkit-animation-direction: reverse;
            animation-direction: reverse;
}
```

Notice the reverse direction.

4. Create the **slide** keyframe.

```
@-webkit-keyframes slide {

    to {
        -webkit-transform: translate(600px, 0px);
          -ms-transform: translate(600px, 0px);
            transform: translate(600px, 0px);
    }

}

@keyframes slide {

    to {
        -webkit-transform: translate(600px, 0px);
          -ms-transform: translate(600px, 0px);
            transform: translate(600px, 0px);
    }

}
```

5. Load your page.

   First it jumps 600 pixels to the right (so fast that you might not see the .box on the left before the jump), and then it slides back to its initial location and repeats the sequence three times.

6. Change the value for the **animation-direction** in step 3 to **alternate** (**EXAMPLE 4.7**).

```
-webkit-animation-direction: alternate;
        animation-direction: alternate;
```

7. Reload your page, and observe the difference (**FIGURE 4.7**).

   Now the .box div slides back and forth between the initial and ending states. This makes for a much smoother overall animation. Experiment with the normal and alternate-reverse values.

FIGURE 4.7
Animation direction

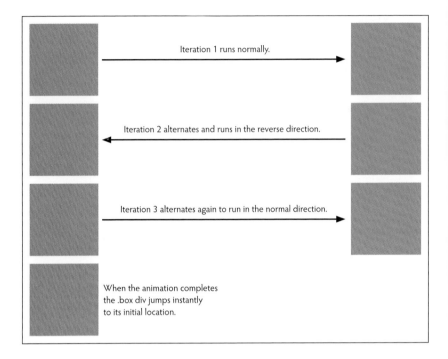

animation-play-state Property

By default, your animations run as soon as the `animation-name` property is assigned. You can change that behavior with the `animation-play-state` property, which defines whether an animation is `running` or `paused`.

```
-webkit-animation-play-state: running;
        animation-play-state: running;


-webkit-animation-play-state: paused;
        animation-play-state: paused;
```

The default value, as you would likely guess, is `running`. If you change the value to `paused`, the animation stops where it is until the `animation-play-state` is changed again to `running`. When `paused`, the animation displays whatever state the animation was in at that moment. When the animation is resumed, it restarts from the state it was paused in.

Let's make one addition to Example 4.7 (**EXAMPLE 4.8**).

1. Add the `animation-play-state` property to the `.box div` from the previous example. Additions to the code are highlighted.

```
.box {
    -webkit-animation-name: slide;
        animation-name: slide;

    -webkit-animation-duration: 5s;
        animation-duration: 5s;

    -webkit-animation-timing-function: linear;
        animation-timing-function: linear;

    -webkit-animation-iteration-count: 3;
        animation-iteration-count: 3;

    -webkit-animation-direction: alternate;
        animation-direction: alternate;

    -webkit-animation-play-state: paused;
        animation-play-state: paused;
}
```

2. Reload your page.

   Unlike previous examples, this time the animation doesn't run when the page is finished loading. To run the animation, you need to change `animation-play-state` to `running` and reload the page.

   This isn't particularly useful if you have to reload the page after changing the `animation-play-state` property, but it becomes much more useful when changing properties via JavaScript or some other trigger.

   Let's modify the example to add triggers.

3. Modify your HTML to include play and pause buttons.

```html
<div class="container">

    <div class="box" id="box"></div>

    <button id="play">Play</button>

    <button id="pause">Pause</button>

</div>
```

The buttons get `id`s so your JavaScript code has something to hook into. Notice that the code adds an `id` of `box` to the `.box div`.

The buttons need some styling.

4. Add the following to your CSS:

```css
button {

    padding: 0.5em 1em;

    border: 1px solid #999;

    border-radius: 5%;

    margin-top: 3em;

}
```

Nothing special. Just a little style to make your buttons look "buttony." Now let's add some JavaScript so the buttons do something.

5. Add the following code in the **head** of your document between `<script>` `</script>` tags.

```html
<script>
var init = function() {

    var box = document.getElementById('box');

    var play = document.getElementById('play');

    var pause = document.getElementById('pause');
```

```
document.getElementById('play').addEventListener(
→ 'click', function(){
    box.style.webkitAnimationPlayState = "running";
    box.style.animationPlayState = "running";
}, false);

document.getElementById('pause').addEventListener(
→ 'click', function(){
    box.style.webkitAnimationPlayState = "paused";
    box.style.animationPlayState = "paused";
}, false);

};

window.addEventListener('DOMContentLoaded', init, false);
</script>
```

Hopefully, the script looks somewhat familiar. The last line of code listens for the page to load and then calls the `init` function.

Inside the function, you first get hooks to each button and the `.box div` and set them to appropriately named variables. Next you add event listeners to each button, and if a button is clicked, you set the value of `animationPlayState` to either `running` or `paused`, depending on which button was clicked.

6. Reload your page one more time.

You should see the new play and pause buttons. The green box sits in the top-left corner until you click the Play button to start the animation. Once the box begins moving, you can click the Pause button to stop the animation. Clicking Play starts the animation again from the point at which it was stopped.

animation-delay Property

The `animation-delay` property defines when an animation starts. It works the same way the `transition-delay` property works. Like `transition-delay`, values are in units of time and can be positive, 0, or negative.

```
-webkit-animation-delay: 2s;
        animation-delay: 2s;

-webkit-animation-delay: 0s;
        animation-delay: 0s;

-webkit-animation-delay: -2s;
        animation-delay: -2s;
```

A positive value delays the animation until some point in the future. A value of 0 (the default) starts the animation instantly. A negative value appears to start the animation in the past. It starts instantly, but at a point in the middle of the animation. The delay works as an offset.

Let's continue to build on Example 4.8.

1. Add an `animation-delay` to the `.box` div. Additions to the code are highlighted (**EXAMPLE 4.9**).

```
.box {
    -webkit-animation-name: slide;
            animation-name: slide;

    -webkit-animation-duration: 5s;
            animation-duration: 5s;

    -webkit-animation-timing-function: linear;
            animation-timing-function: linear;

    -webkit-animation-iteration-count: 3;
            animation-iteration-count: 3;

    -webkit-animation-direction: alternate;
            animation-direction: alternate;
```

```
  -webkit-animation-play-state: running;
        animation-play-state: running;

  -webkit-animation-delay: 2s;
        animation-delay: 2s;
}
```

2. Reload your page.

   The animation does nothing for 2 seconds and then slides back and forth like before (**FIGURE 4.8**). Try using some negative values, and observe the difference.

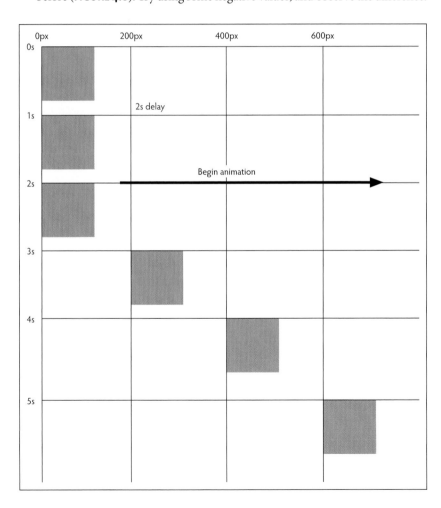

FIGURE 4.8
Animation delay

animation-fill-mode Property

You probably had an idea what each `animation-*` property did before I told you. Some were familiar after working through transitions, and the property names give a pretty good clue about what the others do.

The `animation-fill-mode` property is probably not intuitive to you. You might be thinking about background colors filling your element or something like that. The `animation-fill-mode` property actually defines what values are applied by an animation outside of its execution time.

By default, an animation affects property values only while it's running. This is why the example animations you've been working with often jump back to the initial state when the animation stops. Whatever values are set in each keyframe are the ones used for a property until either the next keyframe changes it or the animation stops playing. When the animation stops, the CSS property values are whatever values were set intrinsically on the element.

The `animation-fill-mode` property overrides this behavior. It takes four keyword values.

`animation-fill-mode: none | forwards | backwards | both`

* `none` is the default, and it doesn't apply any property values in the animation outside the animation's execution.

* `backwards` applies the property values defined in the first keyframe that starts the first iteration to the period defined by `animation-delay`. The values come from either the `0%` (`from`) or `100%` (`to`) keyframes, depending on the value of the `animation-direction` property.

* `forwards` applies the property values after the animation stops. If the `animation-iteration-count` value is greater than 0, the values applied are those at the end of the last completed iteration. If the count value equals 0, the values applied are those that start the first iteration.

* `both` does what you might expect and applies both the `forwards` and `backwards` values to the `animation-fill-mode` property.

Once again let's expand the example we've been working with.

1. Add an `animation-fill-mode` to the `.box` div. Additions to the code are highlighted. Note that the `iteration-count` changes to `1` (**EXAMPLE 4.10**).

```
.box {
    -webkit-animation-name: slide;
            animation-name: slide;

    -webkit-animation-duration: 5s;
            animation-duration: 5s;

    -webkit-animation-timing-function: linear;
            animation-timing-function: linear;

    -webkit-animation-iteration-count: 1;
            animation-iteration-count: 1;

    -webkit-animation-direction: alternate;
            animation-direction: alternate;

    -webkit-animation-play-state: running;
            animation-play-state: running;

    -webkit-animation-delay: 2s;
            animation-delay: 2s;

    -webkit-animation-fill-mode: forwards;
            animation-fill-mode: forwards;
}
```

2. Load the page in a browser.

As before, the green box slides to the right when the animation begins. However, now when it stops it doesn't jump back to its initial state. Setting the `animation-fill-mode` to `forwards` allows the `.box div` to hold the final state in the animation after the animation completes (**FIGURE 4.9**).

FIGURE 4.9
Animation fill mode

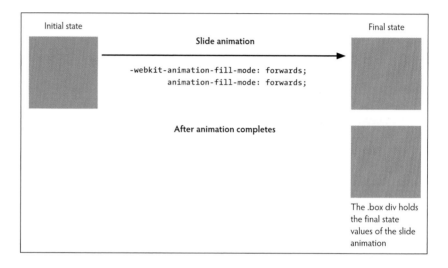

Experiment with the different `animation-fill-mode` values to observe what each does. Change some of the other `animation-*` property values in combination with the `animation-fill-mode` property as well.

For example, use either of the reverse values on the `animation-direction` and then use `forwards` on the `animation-fill-mode`.

```
animation-direction: alternate-reverse;
```

```
animation-fill-mode: backwards;
```

Or add a `0%` (or `from`) keyframe in the `@keyframes` rule so the `.box` begins the animation in a different location.

```
0% {
    -webkit-transform: translate(75px, 0px);
        -ms-transform: translate(75px, 0px);
            transform: translate(75px, 0px);
}
```

Make sure there's a positive `animation-delay`, and set `animation-fill-mode` to `backwards`.

```
animation-fill-mode: backwards;
```

For both changes, observe where the `.box div` is located before and after the animation as well as during the `animation-delay`.

animation Shorthand Property

You can also use the animation shorthand property to set everything at once. You saw this in the first example in this chapter.

```
animation: animation-property animation-duration
→ animation-timing-function animation-delay
→ animation-iteration-count animation-direction
→ animation-fill-mode animation-play-state;
```

If you replace each of the properties with a value, you get something like this:

```
animation: slide 2s ease 0.5s 2 reverse both running;
```

To add multiple animations, you separate each definition with a comma like this:

```
animation: slide 2s ease 0.5s 2 reverse both running,
→ bounce 5s ease-in-out 0 3 alternate forwards paused;
```

Note that the comma occurs between the full definition for each animation. There are two definitions in this line of code, so a single comma between them is all you need.

As with transitions, order is important. Just as with the transition shorthand, the first time value is assigned to the `animation-duration` property, and the second time value is assigned to the `animation-delay` property.

NOTE

The current animation spec mentions a possible future addition. At some point, a / notation might be added to the shorthand. If that happens, you'll be able to specify duration and delay as 10s/2s, where the numerator (10s) is the duration and the denominator (2s) is the delay. This doesn't work now, but is a future possibility.

Animation Events

You learned in the last chapter that when a transition completes, it generates a DOM event. Animations also fire events. They fire an event at the start and end of an animation as well as the end of each iteration.

Types of Animation Events

Transitions fire an event only when the transition ends. Animations can fire any of three possible events:

- An `animationstart` event fires when the animation starts. If a positive `animation-delay` has been set, the event fires when the delay ends. If the delay is negative, the event fires immediately with an `elapsedTime` equal to the absolute value of the delay.

- An `animationend` event fires when the animation completes. This event is similar to the `transitionend` event.

- An `animationiteration` event fires at the end of each iteration of an animation, except the last one when an `animationend` event fires instead. This means animations with zero or one iteration won't fire an `animation-iteration` event.

For transitions the `transitionend` event offers three read-only values. Similarly there are three read-only values you can access with animation events:

- `animationName` is the value of the `animation-name` property of the animation that fired the event.

- `elapsedTime` is the amount of time the animation has been running, in seconds, when this `transitionend` event fires. This time excludes any time the animation was paused. The `elapsedTime` for an `animationstart` event is 0.0s.

- `pseudoElement` is the name (beginning with two colons) of the CSS pseudo-element on which the animation runs or an empty string if the animation runs directly on an element. At the moment only Firefox version 23 and newer supports reading this value, but in practice I've yet to get it working.

Animations can have multiple properties animating at the same time. These can be properties set on a single animation or on multiple animations. An event is generated for each `animation-name` value and not for each individual property being animated.

As long as an animation has a valid `@keyframes` rule and a nonzero duration, it generates events, even if the `@keyframes` rule is empty.

Let's try an example so we can experiment with these events and their associated values. You've been working with variations of the same example. Why stop now? You've made the box slide to the right and most of the time back to the left. Let's add another `@keyframes` rule that generates a downward slide. You'll apply this new rule after the `.box` finishes the slide animation.

The animation will slide to the right, slide back to its initial position, and then slide down and back up again (**EXAMPLE 4.11**).

1. Add `div` with a class of `box` and an `id` of `box` to your HTML.

   The class is used to style the `div` like you've been doing all along, and the `id` is used to hook into the element via JavaScript. The `class` name and `id` name don't need to be the same. You just need to make sure to match the names you give them in the appropriate place in the code.

   ```
   <div class="box" id="box"></div>
   ```

2. Give the `.box div` dimensions and a background color so you can see it on the page, and then add an animation using the animation shorthand.

   ```
   .box {
       width: 200px;
       height: 200px;
       background-color: #393;

       -webkit-animation: slide 2s linear 0s 2 alternate
       → both;
               animation: slide 2s linear 0s 2 alternate
               → both;
   }
   ```

Before creating the `@keyframes` rule, take a look at the shorthand in this code, and make sense of what it's doing. It's calling an `@keyframes` rule named `slide`. Each animation cycle runs a total of 2 seconds. The timing is linear so there is no acceleration. There's no delay, and the animation completes two cycles. It runs once normally and then runs in reverse. Animation elements hold their state both before and after the animation runs.

3. Create the `@keyframes` rule using translation to move the element 600 pixels to the right.

```
@-webkit-keyframes slide {

    100% {
        -webkit-transform: translate(600px, 0px);
            -ms-transform: translate(600px, 0px);
                transform: translate(600px, 0px);
    }

}

@keyframes slide {

    100% {
        -webkit-transform: translate(600px, 0px);
            -ms-transform: translate(600px, 0px);
                transform: translate(600px, 0px);
    }

}
```

4. Load the page in a browser.

The familiar green `.box` slides to the right and then slides back left to its starting point. This animation fires events. You'll capture those events using a little JavaScript. Don't worry, it's no more complicated than what you did in the last chapter with transition events, and you're free to copy the code.

What you're going to do is listen for one of the animation events and when it occurs, start a second animation. The `.box` is probably getting tired of sliding across the page so a `slidedown` `@keyframes` rule seems in order.

5. Create an @**keyframes** rule for a new **slidedown** animation. Add a translation transform, and make the **.box** move 300 pixels down the screen.

```
@-webkit-keyframes slidedown {

    to {
        -webkit-transform: translate(0px, 300px);
          -ms-transform: translate(0px, 300px);
             transform: translate(0px, 300px);
    }
}

@keyframes slidedown {

    to {
        -webkit-transform: translate(0px, 300px);
          -ms-transform: translate(0px, 300px);
             transform: translate(0px, 300px);
    }
}
```

You can reload your page if you'd like, but I'll save the suspense. Nothing changes. You've created a @**keyframe** rule, but it's not attached to any element yet. That's where the events and JavaScript come in.

6. Add the following JavaScript between **<script></script>** tags in the **head** of your document:

```
<script>

var init = function() {
    var box = document.getElementById("box");
```

```
box.addEventListener("webkitAnimationStart",
→ updateAnimation , false);

box.addEventListener("oTAnimationStart",
→ updateAnimation , false);

box.addEventListener("animationstart",
→ updateAnimation , false);


function updateAnimation (e) {

    box.style.webkitAnimationName = "slidedown";

    box.style.animationName = "slidedown";

}

};


window.addEventListener('DOMContentLoaded', init, false);

</script>
```

The JavaScript is a modified version of what you saw with transition events. The last line of code, `window.addEventListener('DOMContentLoaded', init, false);`, once again runs an `init` function after the page content loads.

In the `init` function, you first get the element with an `id` of `box` and assign it to a variable named **box**. Next, you add an event listener (with and without vendor prefixes) to the box to capture an `animationstart` event. When the event is captured, it's passed to an `updateAnimation` function. Finally the `updateAnimation` function changes the `animation-name` value to the `slidedown` animation created in step 5.

7. Reload your page, and observe what happens.

The second animation (`slidedown`) runs, but the first one (`slide`) doesn't. This happens because the JavaScript captures the event that fires at the start of the animation and changes which animation is used before `slide` can run.

Let's capture a different event (**EXAMPLE 4.12**).

8. Change your JavaScript to listen for **animationiteration**, and change its vendor-prefixed variations. Changes in the code are highlighted.

```
<script>

var init = function() {

    var box = document.getElementById("box");

    box.addEventListener("webkitAnimationIteration",
     → updateAnimation , false);

    box.addEventListener("oTAnimationIteration",
     → updateAnimation , false);

    box.addEventListener("animationiteration",
     → updateAnimation , false);

    function updateAnimation (e) {

        box.style.webkitAnimationName = "slidedown";

        box.style.animationName = "slidedown";

    }

};

window.addEventListener('DOMContentLoaded', init, false);

</script>
```

9. Reload your page.

The slide animation starts and completes a single cycle before it jumps back to its initial state and begins and completes both iterations of the **slidedown** animation.

This time you listened for the event that fires at the end of each iteration of an animation. The **slide** animation completes one iteration, the **animationiteration** event is fired, and your code starts the **slidedown** animation. The **slidedown** animation completes because the JavaScript code runs only a single time. No code is listening for the events that the **slidedown** animation fires in this example.

10. Change your JavaScript code to listen for **animationend**, and change its vendor-prefixed variations (**EXAMPLE 4.13**). Changes in the code are highlighted.

```
<script>
var init = function() {
    var box = document.getElementById("box");

    box.addEventListener("webkitAnimationEnd",
      ↦ updateAnimation , false);
    box.addEventListener("oTAnimationEnd",
      ↦ updateAnimation , false);
    box.addEventListener("animationend",
      ↦ updateAnimation , false);

    function updateAnimation (e) {
        box.style.webkitAnimationName = "slidedown";
        box.style.animationName = "slidedown";

    }
};

window.addEventListener('DOMContentLoaded', init, false);
</script>
```

11. Reload the page.

This time both animations start and complete. First **slide** moves the **.box** to the right before returning. As soon as it completes, an **animationend** event is fired. Your JavaScript hears the event and starts the **slidedown** animation, which also completes.

FIGURE 4.10 summarizes listening for each of the three animation events and starting the **slidedown** animation after the **slide** events fire.

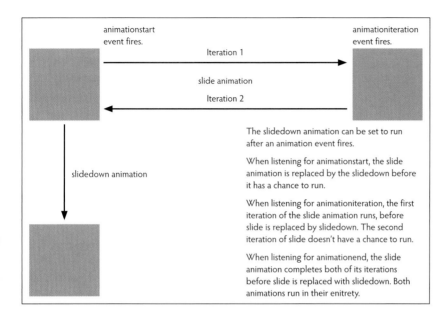

Inside the figure:

animationstart
event fires.

Iteration 1

slide animation

Iteration 2

animationiteration
event fires.

slidedown animation

The slidedown animation can be set to run after an animation event fires.

When listening for animationstart, the slide animation is replaced by the slidedown before it has a chance to run.

When listening for animationiteration, the first iteration of the slide animation runs, before slide is replaced by slidedown. The second iteration of slide doesn't have a chance to run.

When listening for animationend, the slide animation completes both of its iterations before slide is replaced with slidedown. Both animations run in their enitrety.

Let's do one more thing: read the read-only values. You can access and read them at each of the three fired events.

12. Change your JavaScript code to listen for the **animationstart** event, and set an alert to display the **animationName** that fired the event and the **elapsedTime** it's been running. Changes in the code are highlighted.

```
<script>
var init = function() {
    var box = document.getElementById("box");

    box.addEventListener("webkitAnimationStart",
    → updateAnimation , false);

    box.addEventListener("oAnimationStart",
    → updateAnimation , false);

    box.addEventListener("animationstart",
    → updateAnimation , false);
```

```
    function updateAnimation (e) {
        alert("The " + e.animationName + " animation has
        → been running for " + e.elapsedTime + "s");
    }
};


window.addEventListener('DOMContentLoaded', init, false);

</script>
```

13. Reload your page.

As soon as the page loads, the **slide** animation runs, and an alert pops up with the message, "The slide animation has been running for 0s."

FIGURE 4.11 shows the alerts that display when listening for the **animation-iteration** event.

FIGURE 4.11
Animation event read-only
values

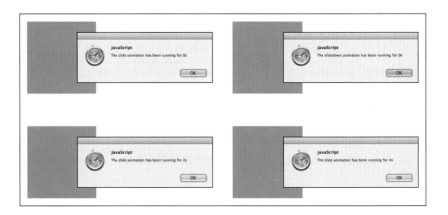

Experiment by changing which event is listened for. Change **animationstart** to **animationiteration**, then to **animationend** (and their vendor-prefixed variants), and observe the differences. When listening for the **animationiteration** event, your alert should read "The slide animation has been running for 2s," and when listening for the **animationend** event it should read "The slide animation has been running for 4s."

Transition or Animation

One of the questions you might be asking yourself is when you should use a transition and when you should use an animation. You can create most of the examples in this and the previous chapter using either transitions or animations. So which should you choose when you want to animate something?

Similarities

You can start to answer that question by thinking about the similarities and differences of transitions and animations. One thing they both have in common is their properties. About half the `animation-*` properties have a counterpart `transition-*` property. The timing functions, for example, are the same, except for using the word `animation` or `transition` to start the property name.

Both can listen for changes to CSS property values and interact with JavaScript events. Triggering events like those in the following list can make changes in CSS property values that start either animations or transitions:

* `:hover`

* `:link`

* `:active`

* `:visited`

* `:focus`

* `:checked`

* `:disabled`

You can also start transitions and animations through changes in media queries or class changes via simple JavaScript that changes the appropriate property values.

Differences

Let's switch gears and think about the differences. Although both transitions and animations can run in response to a trigger, only animations can run automatically on page load. Transitions require a trigger to run. If you need your animation to run automatically, you have only one choice.

Transitions are limited to initial and final state keyframes. Animations can build as many intermediate keyframes as necessary or desired. This gives you more control over your animation and allows you to create more complex and sophisticated animations. Transitions are for simple animations.

Transitions don't change properties. You set values up front in the CSS intrinsic to the specific elements. Transitions define the change only between property values and not the values themselves. Animations can change property values inside each keyframe. The values don't need to be declared outside the animation either, making animation more dynamic.

Transitions can't loop. They run once when triggered and then run in reverse when the trigger is removed. Otherwise they don't run. You can loop animations as many times as you want and set them to run in reverse or alternate between forward and reverse. Once again CSS animations offer you more control than CSS transitions.

Once you start using JavaScript to further control your transitions and animations, it quickly becomes clear that transitions are easier to work with. It's more difficult making changes to the values inside keyframes than it is the intrinsic values on elements.

As a general rule, you'll write more code using CSS animations as opposed to CSS transitions, assuming both are trying to do the same thing.

When you get down to it, animations are abstractions of transitions. States are pulled out from the specific case to work in a more modular fashion. Transitions are a specific case of the more general animation. If you find yourself using the same transition code over and over, you might decide to rewrite it as an animation.

Choosing Transitions or Animations

If what you want to create is a simple animation between two states, keep your code simpler and lighter, or use JavaScript in the animation, then transitions are probably a better choice.

If what you want to create is going to be something more complex with a need for more than two states or if your animation needs to loop or run in either direction and start itself, animations are your choice.

In general, choose CSS transitions for simple animation that require less control, but better integration with JavaScript. Choose CSS animations for more complex and flexible animations that offer you greater control.

There's one question in regard to transitions and animations you might still be wondering about: Does one perform better than the other? To answer that question, let's look at performance.

Performance

The short answer is that you shouldn't see any performance difference between transitions and animations, assuming both are doing the same thing in the same way. Performance has more to do with what properties are being changed as opposed to whether those changes happen through transitions or animations.

To render webpages, a browser first calculates the CSS styles that apply to the HTML elements. Then it lays out the page by working through the geometry and position for each element. Next comes painting where pixels are filled in before finally drawing everything to the screen on composite layers. Browsers use two different execution threads to do all these things and render webpages: the main thread and the compositor thread.

The main thread is responsible for laying out pages and painting elements. It computes the CSS styles applied to HTML elements, and it runs JavaScript. The compositor thread draws bitmaps to the screen via the graphic processing unit (GPU). It determines which parts of the page are visible or will soon be visible. It determines what's likely to be scrolled to next and moves the parts of the page when someone does scroll. Both threads communicate with each other, sending and requesting information.

The main thread tends to be busier for longer periods of time, and while busy it's not responsive to input. The compositor thread, on the other hand, tries to remain responsive because it has to be aware of scrolling.

Main thread responsibilities are more CPU intensive, while compositor responsibilities look to the GPU more frequently. GPUs can draw the same bitmaps over and over in different positions quickly. They can scale and rotate bitmaps quickly as well.

To create more performant animations, you generally want to stay away from layout and painting changes and instead make compositing changes. Compositing changes can be made on separate compositing layers, so the browser doesn't need to repaint or rework the layout of other layers.

TABLE 4.1 lists CSS properties that affect layout and painting.

It turns out that there are currently five things browsers can animate cheaply in terms of performance: translation, scale, rotation, opacity, and some CSS filters. The first three should have you thinking back to transforms. Anything beyond animating these five types of properties probably won't run as smooth.

Consider moving an element to a new location, which is something you've done a few times throughout this book. You can use a transform to move the element, or you can adjust properties like `top` and `left`. The former uses the GPU, while the latter uses the CPU. You want to take advantage of the GPU where possible and take advantage of the hardware acceleration it provides. If you think back to the first example in this chapter, you moved an element by adjusting its `left` value and then by applying a `translation` transform. The approach using `translation` ran smoother, and this is why.

It won't matter whether you use CSS transitions or CSS animations when it comes to performance, but you should think about performance when creating either. Transforms, opacity, and some CSS filters don't require layout or painting changes and so are preferred properties for animating.

This doesn't mean you shouldn't animate other properties. You can still create a smooth animation with other properties. Just realize that if you have the choice, you should opt for changing a transform, opacity, or CSS filter instead of another property.

TABLE 4.1. CSS PROPERTIES

PROPERTIES THAT AFFECT LAYOUT	PROPERTIES THAT AFFECT PAINTING
width	color
height	border-style
padding	border-radius
margin	visibility
display	background
border-width	text-decoration
border	background-size
top	background-image
position	background-position
font-size	background-repeat
float	outline-color
text-align	outline
overflow-y	outline-style
font-weight	outline-width
overflow-y	box-shadow
left	
right	
font-family	
line-height	
vertical-align	
clear	
white-space	
bottom	
min-height	

Summary

In time, you can expect browsers to make more CSS properties quicker to animate. For now, do what you can with what you have. You have enough control over both transitions and animations to animate many CSS properties smoothly and create more realistic-looking animations, which brings us to the next chapter.

CHAPTER 5

MORE REALISTIC ANIMATION

All the animation so far in this book has had a problem. Whether the animation was created using transitions or CSS animations, the problem has been there. It hasn't mattered whether or not the changed properties were transforms or any other CSS property. The problem is that none of the animations to this point have been even remotely realistic.

Boxes sliding across the page or rotating in place aren't realistic or exciting to watch. Even with the smoothest animations and transitions, the objects looked stiff and moved in unnatural ways.

I used simple abstract examples to keep you focused on a new property or the specific value of one property. The unrealistic animations to this point have been to help you learn how to create animations you might actually use.

Simple abstract animations effectively illustrate specific points, but they aren't that interesting once you've learned what they're illustrating. The reasons for more realistic animation include:

* Creating more natural and less robotic and artificial animations
* Creating more engaging and interesting animations
* Creating smoother animations

Compare the animations so far in this book to your favorite cartoon or any cartoon you've seen. Even the most abstract cartoons look far more realistic than anything I've presented up to this point. Let's change that. Let's see if we can create something better, something more natural and realistic.

First we have to learn what makes animation more realistic, and who better to turn to for advice than Disney.

Disney's 12 Principles of Animation

Sometime in the 1930s, Walt Disney wasn't particularly happy with the state of animation at Disney. He thought it was unacceptable for some of the new storylines under construction at the company. He set up classes under the direction of Don Graham for his animators, and from those classes the 12 principles of animation emerged and led to a more natural and realistic way to animate characters.

It wasn't until 1981 that the principles were codified by Disney animators Ollie Johnston and Frank Thomas in their book *Disney Animation: The Illusion of Life* (www.amazon.com/Disney-Animation-The-Illusion-Life/dp/0896592324).

The principles aim to produce the illusion that animated characters follow the laws of physics, making them more realistic and natural. They were the results of observing nature and real life and applying those observations to animation.

In addition to obeying the laws of physics, the 12 principles point the way toward more emotional, interesting, and appealing animations.

The 12 principles aren't meant to be a checklist or recipe to follow. The goal isn't to tick off all the boxes or follow the steps and assume you'll have realistic animation. They're concepts and guidelines to use in different combinations to create more natural animations. They're tools to help you, but they won't create realistic animation for you.

The remainder of this chapter will explore the following 12 principles to help you understand how each can be used to create more realistic animation:

- Squash and stretch
- Anticipation
- Staging
- Straight-ahead action and pose-to-pose action
- Follow-through and overlapping action

- Slow in and slow out
- Arcs
- Secondary action
- Timing
- Exaggeration
- Solid drawing
- Appeal

You'll see how you can code most of the principles, and you'll work to turn a stiff animation into a much more realistic and hopefully interesting one to watch.

Squash and Stretch

Real-world objects have mass and volume. When real objects move, they reveal their rigidity. Squash and stretch shows an object's rigidity by exaggerating its deformation as it moves.

Organic objects aren't completely rigid. They're softer and more malleable. Man-made objects tend to be more stiff and rigid. When organic objects move in a stiff and rigid way, they don't look right. That's not how they behave in real life. Squash and stretch lets the animation respond as the objects would in the real world.

For example, a bouncing ball flattens when it hits the ground (squash) and then elongates (stretch) in the direction it moves after it bounces. How much the ball squashes and stretches depends on its rigidity and its speed and acceleration when it hits the ground and bounces (**FIGURE 5.1**).

The squashing or stretching object should still appear to retain its volume no matter how much squashing and stretching it does. The object is deforming, but it's not losing mass or volume, and its density isn't changing.

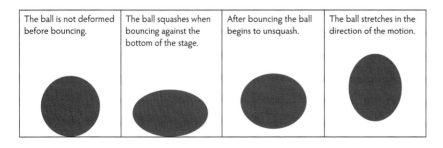

The ball is not deformed before bouncing.	The ball squashes when bouncing against the bottom of the stage.	After bouncing the ball begins to unsquash.	The ball stretches in the direction of the motion.

FIGURE 5.1
Squash and stretch

You can apply squash and stretch to inorganic objects like chairs and tables to help make them appear to have life.

Let's try a squash and stretch example (**EXAMPLE 5.1** through **EXAMPLE 5.3**). You're going to use a bouncing ball throughout this chapter, starting with this example.

1. Add a `div` to your HTML with a class of `ball` and wrap another `div` with a class of `stage` around it.

```
<div class="stage">
    <div class="ball"></div>
</div>
```

The `.stage div` provides a frame for the animation. Because you and I are probably looking at browsers sized to different widths and heights, it would be difficult to use the browser's edge as the "thing" the ball bounces against. By creating a stage for the ball, you can include it in the animation, and we'll both be seeing the same thing.

2. Give your stage dimensions and an outline and then center it on the page. I gave my stage a little top margin to push it away from the browser's edge.

```
.stage {
    width: 1200px;
    height: 600px;
    outline: 1px solid gray;
    margin: 1em auto 0 auto;
}
```

3. Create the ball that you will animate.

```
.ball {
    width: 100px;
    height: 100px;
    border-radius: 50%;
    background: #f00;
    margin: 0 auto;
}
```

You're giving the ball dimensions and a background color in order to see it on the page. The **50% border-radius** on all corners turns what would be a square into a circle, and the **margin** is centering the ball horizontally inside the stage.

4. Add an animation to the ball.

```
.ball {
    -webkit-animation: bounce 2s linear;
            animation: bounce 2s linear;
}
```

Using animation shorthand, you're calling an **@keyframes** rule named **bounce** that will run for 2 seconds with linear timing. Next, you need to code the **@keyframes bounce** rule.

5. Create the **@keyframes bounce** rule and set up a simple, though unrealistic bounce animation.

```
@-webkit-keyframes bounce {

    0% {
    -webkit-transform: translateY(0px);
        -ms-transform: translateY(0px);
            transform: translateY(0px);
    }

    50% {
    -webkit-transform: translateY(500px);
        -ms-transform: translateY(500px);
            transform: translateY(500px);
    }
```

```
    100% {
    -webkit-transform: translateY(0px);
        -ms-transform: translateY(0px);
            transform: translateY(0px);

    }

}

@keyframes bounce {

    0% {
    -webkit-transform: translateY(0px);
        -ms-transform: translateY(0px);
            transform: translateY(0px);
    }

    50% {
    -webkit-transform: translateY(500px);
        -ms-transform: translateY(500px);
            transform: translateY(500px);
    }

    100% {
    -webkit-transform: translateY(0px);
        -ms-transform: translateY(0px);
            transform: translateY(0px);

    }

}
```

6. Load everything into a browser.

You should see a red circle fall from the top of the stage to the bottom where it "bounces" back to the top. Despite its simplicity, you can almost feel it bounce. It's far from realistic, and it's possible that any bounce you see is more wanting to see it than really seeing it. The timing seems unnatural. The ball is rigid. A bouncing ball wouldn't return to its initial height after bouncing.

Let's work on the rigidity problem—that's what squash and stretch is about.

7. Add a `scale` transform to the ball so it squashes when it bounces against the bottom of the stage. Additions to the code are highlighted.

```
@-webkit-keyframes bounce {

    0% {
    -webkit-transform: translateY(0px) scale(1,1);
        -ms-transform: translateY(0px) scale(1,1);
            transform: translateY(0px) scale(1,1);
    }

    50% {
    -webkit-transform: translateY(500px) scale(1.2,0.8);
        -ms-transform: translateY(500px) scale(1.2,0.8);
            transform: translateY(500px) scale(1.2,0.8);
    }

    100% {
    -webkit-transform: translateY(0px) scale(1,1);
        -ms-transform: translateY(0px) scale(1,1);
            transform: translateY(0px) scale(1,1);

    }

}
```

```
@keyframes bounce {

    0% {
    -webkit-transform: translateY(0px) scale(1,1);
        -ms-transform: translateY(0px) scale(1,1);
            transform: translateY(0px) scale(1,1);
    }

    50% {
    -webkit-transform: translateY(500px) scale(1.2,0.8);
        -ms-transform: translateY(500px) scale(1.2,0.8);
            transform: translateY(500px) scale(1.2,0.8);
    }

    100% {
    -webkit-transform: translateY(0px) scale(1,1);
        -ms-transform: translateY(0px) scale(1,1);
            transform: translateY(0px) scale(1,1);
    }

}
```

NOTE

You might be wondering how I arrived at the values 1.2 and 0.8. I guessed. I knew I needed to make the ball wider and shorter, but finding the exact values was trial and error. Don't be afraid to experiment with your CSS property values.

Before reloading the page, think about what you just did. You added a `scale` transform to deform the ball. At the top of the stage (both before and after the bounce) the ball is scaled to its initial size. When it bounces, the ball will become 20 percent wider and 20 percent shorter, appearing to squash.

8. Reload your page and observe the difference adding the `scale` makes.

The ball squashes, but it starts to squash the moment it starts to drop, which doesn't make sense. We'll have to rethink how to set up the squash. And isn't there supposed to be a stretch to go with it?

To save time, step 9 shows the final version of the `@keyframes` rule, which is the result of watching the animation a few times and using trial and error on the values.

9. Replace your `@keyframes` rules with this one:

```
@-webkit-keyframes bounce {

    0% {
    -webkit-transform: translateY(0px) scale(1,1);
        -ms-transform: translateY(0px) scale(1,1);
            transform: translateY(0px) scale(1,1);
    }

    45% {
    -webkit-transform: translateY(500px) scale(1,1);
        -ms-transform: translateY(500px) scale(1,1);
            transform: translateY(500px) scale(1,1);
    }

    50% {
    -webkit-transform: translateY(510px) scale(1.2,0.8);
        -ms-transform: translateY(510px) scale(1.2,0.8);
            transform: translateY(510px) scale(1.2,0.8);

    }

    55% {
    -webkit-transform: translateY(500px) scale(1.1,0.9);
        -ms-transform: translateY(500px) scale(1.1,0.9);
            transform: translateY(500px) scale(1.1,0.9);
    }

    65% {
    -webkit-transform: translateY(350px) scale(0.9,1.1);
        -ms-transform: translateY(350px) scale(0.9,1.1);
```

```
        transform: translateY(350px) scale(0.9,1.1);
    }


    100% {
    -webkit-transform: translateY(0px) scale(1,1);
        -ms-transform: translateY(0px) scale(1,1);
            transform: translateY(0px) scale(1,1);
    }


}

@keyframes bounce {

    0% {
    -webkit-transform: translateY(0px) scale(1,1);
        -ms-transform: translateY(0px) scale(1,1);
            transform: translateY(0px) scale(1,1);
    }

    45% {
    -webkit-transform: translateY(500px) scale(1,1);
        -ms-transform: translateY(500px) scale(1,1);
            transform: translateY(500px) scale(1,1);
    }

    50% {
    -webkit-transform: translateY(510px) scale(1.2,0.8);
        -ms-transform: translateY(510px) scale(1.2,0.8);
            transform: translateY(510px) scale(1.2,0.8);

    }
```

```
55% {
-webkit-transform: translateY(500px) scale(1.1,0.9);
    -ms-transform: translateY(500px) scale(1.1,0.9);
        transform: translateY(500px) scale(1.1,0.9);
}

65% {
-webkit-transform: translateY(350px) scale(0.9,1.1);
    -ms-transform: translateY(350px) scale(0.9,1.1);
        transform: translateY(350px) scale(0.9,1.1);
}

100% {
-webkit-transform: translateY(0px) scale(1,1);
    -ms-transform: translateY(0px) scale(1,1);
        transform: translateY(0px) scale(1,1);
}

}
```

10. Reload your page and observe the changes.

It's not the greatest animation ever created, but it certainly looks more like a bouncing ball than the first time you loaded the page. It squashes as it contacts the floor of the stage and stretches after the bounce. It still has plenty of problems, but you'll fix many before you finish this chapter.

To fix the problem of the ball squashing too soon, you added a couple of keyframes at **45%** and **55%** just before and after the bounce. Heading into the bounce at **45%**, the values are the same as they were at **0%**. At **50%**, the ball is in "full squash mode." Notice that it's set to move 10 pixels farther down, but it doesn't appear to move down in the animation. Scaling to 0.8 in height causes the bottom of the ball to rise 10 pixels, so I compensated by moving the whole ball down the same 10 pixels.

At **55%**, the ball moves back up 10 pixels and starts to scale in reverse. It hasn't quite returned to its initial size, but it is less narrow and squashed than it was at the maximum squash.

I added one more keyframe at **65%** for the stretch. Here the ball deforms to become taller and narrower than it was originally as it bounces back up.

Once again, it's far from amazing animation, but it's an improvement from where you started. There are 11 more principles to help you further improve the animation.

Anticipation

Actions don't start immediately. A good, clear animation lets the viewer know what is about to happen, what is happening, and what just happened. Usually, action in an animation occurs in the following stages and order:

1. Anticipation (setup)

2. Action

3. Follow-through

The setup is anticipation. For example, the act of throwing a ball is preceded by drawing back the arm in a windup before throwing it. The windup is anticipation. It draws your eye to the arm and suggests the arm will then move forward to throw the ball. In this case, the action is physically necessary because you must pull back your arm to throw a ball.

In animation, anticipation leads the viewer's eye to the object that will animate and offer clues for the action that will follow. The faster the action will occur, the longer the anticipation should be. Think of a character slowly forming and holding a pose that precedes them running quickly off the stage in a blur.

Anticipation usually lasts the longest of the three parts of animation. Typically, you'll create more keyframes during anticipation than you will during the action of the animation. With more keyframes, the animation moves slower and seems to last longer. The anticipation directs attention to where the animation will begin, preparing the viewer for a better understanding of what is going on.

The most basic way to include anticipation is through contrary movement or movement in the opposite direction than the main action. Again think of the windup before throwing a ball. The windup moves in the opposite direction of the throw.

Contrary movement is not the only way to show anticipation. You might contract an object before expanding it (**FIGURE 5.2**). A character might look off-screen in anticipation of the action's location or perhaps toward an action approaching the screen.

| The ball is not deformed before the anticipation begins. | Prior to falling, the ball squashes in the opposite direction of the cell to create anticipation. | The ball recoils from its squash and starts to stretch in the direction of the fall. |

FIGURE 5.2
Anticipation

Every major action in an animation or series of animations should include anticipation. The greater the action, the longer and more exaggerated the anticipation should be. At times, a major action might include several smaller setup actions.

Let's see if we can create some anticipation for the bouncing ball (**EXAMPLE 5.4**).

1. Add some keyframes to create anticipation for the bounce. Replace your **bounce @keyframes** rule with the following one. The new keyframes at **10%**, **15%**, **20%**, and **25%** are all highlighted.

```
@-webkit-keyframes bounce {

    0% {
    -webkit-transform: translateY(0px) scale(1,1);
       -ms-transform: translateY(0px) scale(1,1);
           transform: translateY(0px) scale(1,1);
    }
```

```
10% {
-webkit-transform: translateY(-20px) scale(1.4,0.6);
    -ms-transform: translateY(-20px) scale(1.4,0.6);
        transform: translateY(-20px) scale(1.4,0.6);
}

15% {
-webkit-transform: translateY(-22px)
↪ scale(1.44,0.56);
    -ms-transform: translateY(-22px)
    ↪ scale(1.44,0.56);
        transform: translateY(-22px)
        ↪ scale(1.44,0.56);
}

20% {
-webkit-transform: translateY(-20px) scale(1.4,0.6);
    -ms-transform: translateY(-20px) scale(1.4,0.6);
        transform: translateY(-20px) scale(1.4,0.6);
}

25% {
-webkit-transform: translateY(5px) scale(0.9,1.1);
    -ms-transform: translateY(5px) scale(0.9,1.1);
        transform: translateY(5px) scale(0.9,1.1);
}

45% {
-webkit-transform: translateY(500px) scale(1,1);
    -ms-transform: translateY(500px) scale(1,1);
        transform: translateY(500px) scale(1,1);
}
```

```
    50% {

    -webkit-transform: translateY(520px) scale(1.4,0.6);

        -ms-transform: translateY(510px) scale(1.2,0.8);

            transform: translateY(510px) scale(1.2,0.8);


    }


    55% {

    -webkit-transform: translateY(500px) scale(1.1,0.9);

        -ms-transform: translateY(500px) scale(1.1,0.9);

            transform: translateY(500px) scale(1.1,0.9);

    }


    65% {

    -webkit-transform: translateY(350px) scale(0.8,1.2);

        -ms-transform: translateY(350px) scale(0.9,1.1);

            transform: translateY(350px) scale(0.9,1.1);

    }


    100% {

    -webkit-transform: translateY(0px) scale(1,1);

        -ms-transform: translateY(0px) scale(1,1);

            transform: translateY(0px) scale(1,1);

    }


}


@keyframes bounce {

    0% {

    -webkit-transform: translateY(0px) scale(1,1);

        -ms-transform: translateY(0px) scale(1,1);
```

```
            transform: translateY(0px) scale(1,1);
}

10% {
-webkit-transform: translateY(-20px) scale(1.4,0.6);
    -ms-transform: translateY(-20px) scale(1.4,0.6);
        transform: translateY(-20px)
        → scale(1.4,0.6);
}

15% {
-webkit-transform: translateY(-22px)
→ scale(1.44,0.56);
    -ms-transform: translateY(-22px)
    → scale(1.44,0.56);
        transform: translateY(-22px)
        → scale(1.44,0.56);
}

20% {
-webkit-transform: translateY(-20px) scale(1.4,0.6);
    -ms-transform: translateY(-20px) scale(1.4,0.6);
        transform: translateY(-20px) scale(1.4,0.6);
}

25% {
-webkit-transform: translateY(0px) scale(0.9,1.1);
    -ms-transform: translateY(0px) scale(0.9,1.1);
        transform: translateY(0px) scale(0.9,1.1);
}

45% {
-webkit-transform: translateY(500px) scale(1,1);
```

```
      -ms-transform: translateY(500px) scale(1,1);
         transform: translateY(500px) scale(1,1);

}


50% {

-webkit-transform: translateY(510px) scale(1.2,0.8);

   -ms-transform: translateY(510px) scale(1.2,0.8);

      transform: translateY(510px) scale(1.2,0.8);


}


55% {

-webkit-transform: translateY(500px) scale(1.1,0.9);

   -ms-transform: translateY(500px) scale(1.1,0.9);

      transform: translateY(500px) scale(1.1,0.9);

}


65% {

-webkit-transform: translateY(350px) scale(0.9,1.1);

   -ms-transform: translateY(350px) scale(0.9,1.1);

      transform: translateY(350px) scale(0.9,1.1);

}


100% {

-webkit-transform: translateY(0px) scale(1,1);

   -ms-transform: translateY(0px) scale(1,1);

      transform: translateY(0px) scale(1,1);

}


}
```

2. Reload your page and take a look at the anticipation you created.

You added four keyframes to the start of the **@keyframes** rule that together take up 25 percent of the animation. The ball first squashes, but apparently under its own power as though it's a spring coiling. The tweaked values in the **15%** keyframe make the ball hold the squash a little longer than needed. At **25%**, the ball elongates and is about to start its fall to the bottom of the stage.

Speaking of the stage…

Staging

Staging provides context for the animation. It's what the simple stage in the examples so far has been doing.

Staging is how you pose objects and how you let the action unfold. Staging is about communication. For example, consider the two views of the object in **FIGURE 5.3**. The view on the left shows the object as a 3-dimensional cube. The view on the right shows only a single face of the box making it look like a 2-dimensional square. The decision to show one view over the other helps stage the object.

FIGURE 5.3
Staging

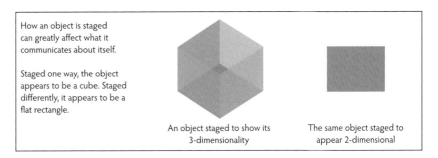

How an object is staged can greatly affect what it communicates about itself.

Staged one way, the object appears to be a cube. Staged differently, it appears to be a flat rectangle.

An object staged to show its 3-dimensionality

The same object staged to appear 2-dimensional

You should consider three things when staging:

- ◆ Character
- ◆ Environment
- ◆ Action

Characters and objects should have strong silhouettes to give them an easily and quickly understood pose. As an animator, you must see the form in an object. You should choose the best angle to show the form and remove details from the object while still clearly communicating its pose.

The environment (the stage) should be interesting and alive. You should create realistic-looking backgrounds that observe the rules of physics established by the animation. Background characters and objects should also seem alive, although they should not steal the attention away from the main object or action.

Major actions should happen one at a time. If too much is happening at once, viewers may be confused as where to look when minor actions upstage the major action.

Staging done well helps tell the animation story: It contributes to the central idea, sets the context, and adds to the atmosphere. Composition, the play of light over objects, color, the pose of objects, and the flow and rhythm of movement all contribute to the staging.

Let's add some context to the ball animation by adding a few details to the stage (**EXAMPLE 5.5**).

1. Add a `div` with a class of **floor** to your HTML.

```
<div class="stage ">
    <div class="ball"></div>
    <div class="floor"></div>
</div>
```

You're going to style the stage (and floor) so the ball appears to be bouncing in the interior of a room.

2. Give the `.stage` a background color. Set its position to **relative** and give it a **z-index** of **-10**. Here are all the styles you should now have on the `.stage` class. The additions to the code are highlighted.

```
.stage  {
    width: 1200px;
    height: 600px;
    outline: 1px solid gray;
    margin: 1em auto 0 auto;

    position: relative;
    z-index: -10;
    background: #ddf;
}
```

The background color is a light blue. The positioning and negative **z-index** are needed for what you're about to set on the `.floor` class.

3. Create the `.floor` class in your CSS and add the following styles:

```
.floor {
    position: absolute;
    top: 80%;
    z-index: -1;
    width: 100%;
    height: 20%;
    background-color: #876;
    background-image:
        repeating-linear-gradient(45deg, transparent,
        → transparent 15px,
        rgba(255,255,255,.5) 15px,
        rgba(255,255,255,.5) 30px);
}
```

The floor should fill the bottom of the stage. I chose to have the floor take up the bottom 20 percent of the stage, which led to the values for `height: 20%`, `top: 80%`, and `width: 100%`. The floor is positioned inside the stage, which is why the stage needed relative positioning. The floor also gets a `z-index` of `-1`, which places it closer to the viewer than the stage but behind the bouncing ball.

For a background, I chose to customize a CSS background pattern that I found on Lea Verou's CSS3 Pattern Gallery site (http://lea.verou.me/css3patterns).

There's one last thing to do before checking the page in your browser.

4. Nudge the location of the bounce up by changing the value of the translate function at the **45%**, **50%**, and **55%** keyframes. Here's what the keyframes should look like:

```
45% {
    -webkit-transform: translateY(450px) scale(0.9,1.1);
        -ms-transform: translateY(450px) scale(1,1);
            transform: translateY(450px) scale(1,1);
}
```

```
50% {

    -webkit-transform: translateY(460px) scale(1.2,0.8);

        -ms-transform: translateY(460px) scale(1.2,0.8);

            transform: translateY(460px) scale(1.2,0.8);


}

55% {

    -webkit-transform: translateY(450px) scale(1.1,0.9);

        -ms-transform: translateY(450px) scale(1.1,0.9);

            transform: translateY(450px) scale(1.1,0.9);

}
```

Here I moved the location where the ball bounces up by 50 pixels. It's not a lot, but it should give the perception that the ball is bouncing on the floor and not against the edge of an arbitrary frame.

5. Reload your page and watch the latest version of the animation.

You didn't change much on the motion, and I'll be the first to admit that the styles for the `.stage` and `.floor` are amateurish at best. Still, the stage has been set, and the ball appears to be bouncing in some kind of physical space as opposed to inside an abstract frame (**FIGURE 5.4**).

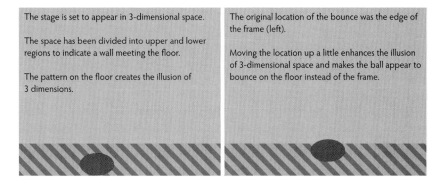

The stage is set to appear in 3-dimensional space.

The space has been divided into upper and lower regions to indicate a wall meeting the floor.

The pattern on the floor creates the illusion of 3 dimensions.

The original location of the bounce was the edge of the frame (left).

Moving the location up a little enhances the illusion of 3-dimensional space and makes the ball appear to bounce on the floor instead of the frame.

FIGURE 5.4
Staging

Straight-Ahead Action and Pose-to-Pose Action

This principle refers to the methods of creating animation. In *straight-ahead action*, an animator draws everything in frame one, then proceeds to draw everything in frame two, and so on in sequence until the last frame is drawn. Think of a flip book as an example of this kind of animation.

This method is an explorative kind of process and tends to lead to more creative animation, but it can be difficult to time correctly and modify later. There's probably little advanced planning for the entire animation. The animator might have no idea how the animation will turn out when drawing the first frame.

Straight-ahead action is the approach beginner animators typically use. It's the natural and spontaneous approach and is the better approach when the animation will be complex and dynamic.

Pose-to-pose action is created by drawing the key poses and frames and then creating the in-between frames to connect them. Computers use this approach, because they are much quicker at creating in-between frames.

This method works well when you need a specific timing to occur at specific points. It's also good for planning the animation in advance, and it's easier to modify. Pose-to-pose action establishes a framework of key moments or keyframes and is usually the better approach for simple animations.

Pose-to-pose is the method for all the animations in this book. It's the method you'll most likely use for all the animation you create on a website.

Follow-through and Overlapping Action

Earlier I mentioned that animations occur in order over three different sections: the setup, the action itself, and the follow-through. Anticipation is the setup. Guess which of the three the principle of follow-through and overlapping action is concerned with?

Follow-through is similar to anticipation, except that it comes at the end of the animation. Just as animations don't begin suddenly, they don't end suddenly. More likely, the animated object moves past its eventual resting point before coming back to rest. After the object has come to rest, maybe parts of it continue to wiggle, wave about, or react momentarily as if bouncing between two springs.

For example, when throwing a ball, your arm doesn't stop moving the moment you let go of the ball. Your arm continues its motion, going past the point where the ball is released.

I've never bounced a ball only to have it come to rest at the top of the bounce. Every ball I've bounced on the ground bounces a few times, each bounce a little less than the previous one, until the ball eventually comes to rest. All those extra bounces are follow-through.

1. Replace your **@keyframes** rules with the following. It has a few more keyframes than the rules you've used so far. I've added comments so you can map the keyframes to the bounce animation (**EXAMPLE 5.6**).

```
@-webkit-keyframes bounce {

    /* ---------------------------------------------- */
    /* -- ANTICIPATION
    /* ---------------------------------------------- */
    0% {
        -webkit-transform: translateY(0px) scale(1,1);
           -ms-transform: translateY(0px) scale(1,1);
               transform: translateY(0px) scale(1,1);
    }

    10%  {
        -webkit-transform: translateY(-20px)
        → scale(1.4,0.6);
           -ms-transform: translateY(-20px)
           → scale(1.4,0.6);
               transform: translateY(-20px)
               → scale(1.4,0.6);
    }
```

```
15%  {
    -webkit-transform: translateY(-22px)
    → scale(1.44,0.56);

        -ms-transform: translateY(-22px)
        → scale(1.44,0.56);

            transform: translateY(-22px)
            → scale(1.44,0.56);

}


20%  {
    -webkit-transform: translateY(-20px)
    → scale(1.4,0.6);

        -ms-transform: translateY(-20px)
        → scale(1.4,0.6);

            transform: translateY(-20px)
            → scale(1.4,0.6);

}


25%  {
    -webkit-transform: translateY(0px) scale(1,1);

        -ms-transform: translateY(0px) scale(1,1);

            transform: translateY(0px) scale(1,1);

}




/* ---------------------------------------------- */
/* -- FIRST BOUNCE
/* ---------------------------------------------- */
35%  {
    -webkit-transform: translateY(450px)
    → scale(0.9,1.1);

        -ms-transform: translateY(450px)
        → scale(0.9,1.1);
```

```
        transform: translateY(450px)
        ↪ scale(0.9,1.1);

}

40%  {

    -webkit-transform: translateY(460px)
    ↪ scale(1.2,0.8);

        -ms-transform: translateY(460px)
        ↪ scale(1.2,0.8);

            transform: translateY(460px)
            ↪ scale(1.2,0.8);

}

45%  {

    -webkit-transform: translateY(450px)
    ↪ scale(1.1,0.9);

        -ms-transform: translateY(450px)
        ↪ scale(1.1,0.9);

            transform: translateY(450px)
            ↪ scale(1.1,0.9);

}




/* ------------------------------------------------ */
/* -- RETURN
/* ------------------------------------------------ */

62%  {

    -webkit-transform: translateY(275px)
    ↪ scale(0.95,1.05);

        -ms-transform: translateY(250px)
        ↪ scale(0.95,1.05);

            transform: translateY(250px)
            ↪ scale(0.95,1.05);

}
```

```
65%  {

    -webkit-transform: translateY(250px) scale(1,1);

        -ms-transform: translateY(250px) scale(1,1);

            transform: translateY(250px) scale(1,1);

}



68%  {

    -webkit-transform: translateY(275px)
    → scale(0.95,1.05);

        -ms-transform: translateY(250px)
        → scale(0.95,1.05);

            transform: translateY(250px)
            → scale(0.95,1.05);

}



/* ---------------------------------------------- */
/* -- SECOND BOUNCE
/* ---------------------------------------------- */
75%  {

    -webkit-transform: translateY(450px)
    → scale(0.95,1.05);

        -ms-transform: translateY(450px)
        → scale(0.95,1.05);

            transform: translateY(450px)
            → scale(0.95,1.05);

}



78%  {

    -webkit-transform: translateY(460px)
    → scale(1.1,0.9);

        -ms-transform: translateY(460px)
        → scale(1.1,0.9);
```

```
            transform: translateY(460px)
             ↪ scale(1.1,0.9);
}


82%  {

    -webkit-transform: translateY(450px)
     ↪ scale(0.95,1.05);

        -ms-transform: translateY(450px)
         ↪ scale(0.95,1.05);

            transform: translateY(450px)
             ↪ scale(0.95,1.05);
}



/* ---------------------------------------------- */
/* -- RETURN
/* ---------------------------------------------- */

86%  {

    -webkit-transform: translateY(400px)
     ↪ scale(0.95,1.05);

        -ms-transform: translateY(400px)
         ↪ scale(0.95,1.05);

            transform: translateY(400px)
             ↪ scale(0.95,1.05);
}



/* ---------------------------------------------- */
/* -- THIRD BOUNCE
/* ---------------------------------------------- */

90%  {

    -webkit-transform: translateY(400px)
     ↪ scale(0.9,1.1);
```

```
            -ms-transform: translateY(400px)
         → scale(0.9,1.1);

            transform: translateY(400px)
          → scale(0.9,1.1);

}


94% {

    -webkit-transform: translateY(450px) scale(1,1);

        -ms-transform: translateY(450px) scale(1,1);

            transform: translateY(450px) scale(1,1);

}


98% {

    -webkit-transform: translateY(460px) scale(1,1);

        -ms-transform: translateY(460px) scale(1,1);

            transform: translateY(460px) scale(1,1);

}



/* --------------------------------------------- */
/* -- REST
/* --------------------------------------------- */
100% {

    -webkit-transform: translateY(460px) scale(1,1);

        -ms-transform: translateY(460px) scale(1,1);

            transform: translateY(460px) scale(1,1);

}


}
```

```
@keyframes bounce {

    /* -------------------------------------------- */
    /* -- ANTICIPATION
    /* -------------------------------------------- */
    0% {

        -webkit-transform: translateY(0px) scale(1,1);

            -ms-transform: translateY(0px) scale(1,1);

                transform: translateY(0px) scale(1,1);

    }


    10%  {

        -webkit-transform: translateY(-20px)
        ↪ scale(1.4,0.6);

            -ms-transform: translateY(-20px)
            ↪ scale(1.4,0.6);

                transform: translateY(-20px)
                ↪ scale(1.4,0.6);

    }


    15%  {

        -webkit-transform: translateY(-22px)
        ↪ scale(1.44,0.56);

            -ms-transform: translateY(-22px)
            ↪ scale(1.44,0.56);

                transform: translateY(-22px)
                ↪ scale(1.44,0.56);

    }


    20%  {

        -webkit-transform: translateY(-20px)
        ↪ scale(1.4,0.6);

            -ms-transform: translateY(-20px)
            ↪ scale(1.4,0.6);
```

```
            transform: translateY(-20px)
             ↪ scale(1.4,0.6);
}


25%  {

    -webkit-transform: translateY(0px) scale(1,1);
        -ms-transform: translateY(0px) scale(1,1);
            transform: translateY(0px) scale(1,1);
}




/* ---------------------------------------------- */
/* -- FIRST BOUNCE
/* ---------------------------------------------- */
35%  {

    -webkit-transform: translateY(450px)
     ↪ scale(0.9,1.1);
        -ms-transform: translateY(450px)
         ↪ scale(0.9,1.1);
            transform: translateY(450px)
             ↪ scale(0.9,1.1);
}


40%  {

    -webkit-transform: translateY(460px)
     ↪ scale(1.2,0.8);
        -ms-transform: translateY(460px)
         ↪ scale(1.2,0.8);
            transform: translateY(460px)
             ↪ scale(1.2,0.8);
}
```

```
45%  {

    -webkit-transform: translateY(450px)
    ⤷ scale(1.1,0.9);

        -ms-transform: translateY(450px)
        ⤷ scale(1.1,0.9);

            transform: translateY(450px)
            ⤷ scale(1.1,0.9);

}




/* --------------------------------------------- */

/* -- RETURN

/* --------------------------------------------- */

62%  {

    -webkit-transform: translateY(275px)
    ⤷ scale(0.95,1.05);

        -ms-transform: translateY(250px)
        ⤷ scale(0.95,1.05);

            transform: translateY(250px)
            ⤷ scale(0.95,1.05);

}


65%  {

    -webkit-transform: translateY(250px) scale(1,1);

        -ms-transform: translateY(250px) scale(1,1);

            transform: translateY(250px) scale(1,1);

}
```

```
68%  {

    -webkit-transform: translateY(275px)
    → scale(0.95,1.05);

        -ms-transform: translateY(250px)
        → scale(0.95,1.05);

            transform: translateY(250px)
            → scale(0.95,1.05);

}



/* -------------------------------------------- */

/* -- SECOND BOUNCE

/* -------------------------------------------- */

75%  {

    -webkit-transform: translateY(450px)
    → scale(0.95,1.05);

        -ms-transform: translateY(450px)
        → scale(0.95,1.05);

            transform: translateY(450px)
            → scale(0.95,1.05);

}


78%  {

    -webkit-transform: translateY(460px)
    → scale(1.1,0.9);

        -ms-transform: translateY(460px)
        → scale(1.1,0.9);

            transform: translateY(460px)
            → scale(1.1,0.9);

}
```

```
82%  {

     -webkit-transform: translateY(450px)
     → scale(0.95,1.05);

        -ms-transform: translateY(450px)
        → scale(0.95,1.05);

           transform: translateY(450px)
           → scale(0.95,1.05);

}



/* ---------------------------------------------- */

/* -- RETURN

/* ---------------------------------------------- */

86%  {

     -webkit-transform: translateY(400px)
     → scale(0.95,1.05);

        -ms-transform: translateY(400px)
        → scale(0.95,1.05);

           transform: translateY(400px)
           → scale(0.95,1.05);

}



/* ---------------------------------------------- */

/* -- THIRD BOUNCE

/* ---------------------------------------------- */

90%  {

     -webkit-transform: translateY(400px)
     → scale(0.9,1.1);

        -ms-transform: translateY(400px)
        → scale(0.9,1.1);

           transform: translateY(400px)
           → scale(0.9,1.1);

}
```

```
94% {
        -webkit-transform: translateY(450px) scale(1,1);
           -ms-transform: translateY(450px) scale(1,1);
               transform: translateY(450px) scale(1,1);
}

98% {
        -webkit-transform: translateY(460px) scale(1,1);
           -ms-transform: translateY(460px) scale(1,1);
               transform: translateY(460px) scale(1,1);
}



/* ---------------------------------------------- */
/* -- REST
/* ---------------------------------------------- */
100% {
        -webkit-transform: translateY(460px) scale(1,1);
           -ms-transform: translateY(460px) scale(1,1);
               transform: translateY(460px) scale(1,1);
}


}
```

2. Reload your page with this new @keyframes rule and watch the animation (**FIGURE 5.5**).

Everything after the first bounce is follow-through. In fact, most of the action is follow-through. It's still pretty amateurish as far as animations go, but it's a lot more realistic than where you started.

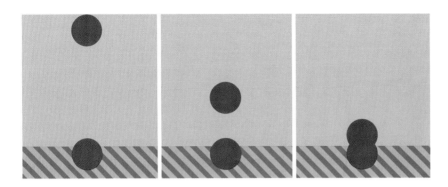

FIGURE 5.5
Follow-through

Overlapping action is the second part of this principle, and it refers to any additional action that occurs as a result of the main action. For example, the ears of an animated rabbit probably swing while the rabbit is hopping around. The hopping is the main action, and the flapping ears are the overlapping action. The main action causes the overlapping action.

Overlapping actions might have different timing, and they might move at different speeds from the main action and each other. Overlapping action helps maintain the flow between an animation starting and stopping. Combined, the main action and any overlapping actions help create the impression that the object is following the laws of physics. It's the movement at different speeds and timing that gives this impression.

Overlapping actions shouldn't have to wait for one another or the main action to stop before they can begin. Overlapping actions usually happen at the same time as the main action. The start of one overlaps the end of another, and together all the overlapping actions help make up the main action.

In some sense the squashing and stretching on the ball might be considered overlapping action since it occurs as a result of the movement of the ball. A better example would be if we gave the ball a face and added some arms and legs that flapped about during the bounce animation.

Slow In and Slow Out (Ease In and Out)

An object doesn't go from rest to top speed instantly. It accelerates to top speed and decelerates to zero before coming to rest. Typically, objects move slower at the start and end of any action and gradually accelerate or decelerate.

Think of your car. You don't press the gas pedal and find the car instantly going 60 miles per hour. You accelerate from 0 mph to reach your top speed and then apply the brakes and decelerate back to 0.

This principle starts and stops action at a slower speed than the middle of the action when it's running at a greater speed. You want to ease in to the animation and then ease out at the end, and you want to do the same at key points throughout the animation—your animation will look more realistic.

A simple strategy for slow in, slow out is to add more frames at the beginning and end of an animation (and key actions) and fewer in the middle. This will slow down your animation at the end points and speed it up in the middle.

The bounce animation is already following this principle. When you added the extra keyframes at the beginning for anticipation and added extra keyframes at the end for follow-through, you slowed the action at both the start and end of the animation. You also created additional keyframes around each bounce, which slows the action into the bounce and speeds it up coming out.

Arcs

Until now, all the movement in the animation has been in a straight line. Most movement in the natural world follows an arc. Think about your own body for a moment. Parts of you are connected to other parts of you at your joints. Your joints allow rotational motion, which means your movements end up as arcs. It's similar for nearly everything in the natural world.

It's rare for organic objects to move in a perfectly straight line. You generally want the movement in your animation to follow arcs instead of straight lines for realistic animation. The exception is mechanical movement, which is typically straight—an example of humankind versus nature.

Arcs are so important for motion that traditional animators used to draw them lightly for reference and erase them later when they no longer needed the reference. Using the lightly drawn lines ensured moving objects followed the arcs.

An object in motion will appear erratic if it veers off its natural arc—unless it's acted on by some outside force.

As the speed of an object increases, the arc it follows flattens out. The faster an object is moving, the harder it is for that object to turn, whereas a slower moving object can follow a more pronounced arc.

Keep in mind that the arc of motion can be around any axis. The top of the arc could be the point the arc is closest to the viewer, and the points at its base could be farthest away from the viewer. The top of the arc doesn't have to be up.

The motions in the ball example have been straight lines up to this point. Working some arcs into it is going to require some major reworking (**EXAMPLE 5.7**). Let me describe what you're going to create before I get to the code.

Instead of falling straight down, the ball is now going to roll off a table-like object and bounce across the floor until it contacts a wall. At that point the ball will reverse its direction and rotation and come to rest against a stopper on the floor. That sounds like a lot to do, so let's get started.

1. Add the following code to a new HTML file:

```
<div class="stage ">
    <div class="ball"></div>
    <div class="floor"></div>
    <div class="table"></div>
    <div class="wall"></div>
    <div class="stopper"></div>
</div>
```

Once again your animation is framed inside a stage. A few more objects are inside the stage now. Each will be structured as an empty **div** with a class name that describes the object.

2. Add some CSS styles to set the stage:

```
.stage  {
    width: 1200px;
    height: 600px;
    outline: 1px solid gray;
    margin: 1em auto 0 auto;
```

```
    position: relative;

    z-index: -10;

    background: #ddf;

}

.floor {

    position: absolute;

    top: 80%;

    z-index: -1;

    width: 100%;

    height: 20%;

    background-color: #876;

    background-image:

        repeating-linear-gradient(45deg, transparent,
        → transparent 15px,

        rgba(255,255,255,.5) 15px,

        rgba(255,255,255,.5) 30px);

}

.table {

    position: absolute;

    top: 150px;

    left: 0;

    width: 300px;

    height: 400px;

    background: #00f;

}

.wall {

    position: absolute;
```

```css
    width: 50px;
    height: 500px;
    top: 50px;
    left: 1000px;
    background: #0f0;
}

.stopper {
    position: absolute;
    width: 100px;
    height: 50px;
    top: 500px;
    left: 375px;
    background: #f00;
}

.ball {
    background: #f00;
    position: absolute;
    z-index: 10;
    top: 50px;
    left: 100px;

    width: 0px;
    height: 0px;
    border-width: 50px;
    border-style: solid;;
    border-color: #393 #933 #399 #993;
    border-radius: 50%;
}
```

The stage and the floor are the same as they were earlier. Let's focus on what's new. The table, wall, and stopper are all pretty similar and don't look like what their names imply—they're more abstract. Each is a rectangle of different dimensions, orientation, color, and location.

The ball is borrowed from the previous chapter. It has no width and no height, but its borders do. Each border is a different color, and the overall appearance will be a circle with four evenly divided pie wedges. Let's pretend it's a beach ball. Initially, the ball is located on top of the table.

If you load your page in a browser, nothing will happen, but you'll see the stage is set (**FIGURE 5.6**).

3. Add an animation to the `.ball` class. Additions to the code are highlighted.

```
.ball {
    background: #f00;
    position: absolute;
    z-index: 10;
    top: 50px;
    left: 100px;

    width: 0px;
    height: 0px;
    border-width: 50px;
```

```
border-style: solid;;
border-color: #393 #933 #399 #993;
border-radius: 50%;

-webkit-animation: bounce 2s ease-in-out both;
        animation: bounce 2s ease-in-out both;
}
```

Once again you're calling an **@keyframes** rule named **bounce**. The animation runs for 2 seconds with **ease-in-out** timing. It holds the animation values before and after the animation runs. This particular animation doesn't need to hold its values before the animation, but it does need to hold them after to give the appearance the ball has come to rest in a new location. Otherwise, after it came to rest the ball would instantly jump back onto the table.

All that's left is to create the **@keyframes** rule. It's quite a bit longer than those you've been working with so far. In an effort to save some space, I'll present the non-vendor-prefixed version of the rule. Just remember you need the **@-webkit-keyframes** version as well.

4. Add the **bounce @keyframes** rule.

```
@keyframes bounce {

    0% {
    -webkit-transform: translateX(0) translateY(0px)
    → scale(1,1) rotate(90deg);
        -ms-transform: translateX(0) translateY(0px)
        → scale(1,1) rotate(90deg);
            transform: translateX(0) translateY(0px)
            → scale(1,1) rotate(90deg);
    }

    15% {
    -webkit-transform: translateX(-100px)
    → translateY(0px) scale(1,1) rotate(-90deg);
```

```
        -ms-transform: translateX(-100px)
     → translateY(0px) scale(1,1) rotate(-90deg);

          transform: translateX(-100px)
       → translateY(0px) scale(1,1) rotate(-90deg);

}


25% {

-webkit-transform: translateX(-110px)
 → translateY(-10px) scale(0.8,1.2) rotate(-90deg);

    -ms-transform: translateX(-110px)
     → translateY(-10px) scale(0.8,1.2)
     → rotate(-90deg);

          transform: translateX(-110px)
       → translateY(-10px) scale(0.8,1.2)
       → rotate(-90deg);

}


27% {

-webkit-transform: translateX(-110px)
 → translateY(-10px) scale(0.8,1.2) rotate(-90deg);

    -ms-transform: translateX(-110px)
     → translateY(-10px) scale(0.8,1.2)
     → rotate(-90deg);

          transform: translateX(-110px)
       → translateY(-10px) scale(0.8,1.2)
       → rotate(-90deg);

}


28% {

-webkit-transform: translateX(-100px) translateY(0px)
 → scale(1,1) rotate(-75deg);

    -ms-transform: translateX(-100px) translateY(0px)
     → scale(1,1) rotate(-75deg);

          transform: translateX(-100px) translateY(0px)
       → scale(1,1) rotate(-75deg);

}
```

```
31% {

-webkit-transform: translateX(0px) translateY(0px)
→ scale(1,1) rotate(90deg);

    -ms-transform: translateX(0px) translateY(0px)
    → scale(1,1) rotate(90deg);

        transform: translateX(0px) translateY(0px)
        → scale(1,1) rotate(90deg);

}



35% {

-webkit-transform: translateX(100px) translateY(0px)
→ scale(1,1) rotate(180deg);

    -ms-transform: translateX(100px) translateY(0px)
    → scale(1,1) rotate(180deg);

        transform: translateX(100px) translateY(0px)
        → scale(1,1) rotate(180deg);

}


40% {

-webkit-transform: translateX(200px) translateY(0px)
→ scale(1,1) rotate(270deg);

    -ms-transform: translateX(200px) translateY(0px)
    → scale(1,1) rotate(270deg);

        transform: translateX(200px) translateY(0px)
        → scale(1,1) rotate(270deg);

}


45% {

-webkit-transform: translateX(300px)
→ translateY(135px) scale(1,1) rotate(360deg);

    -ms-transform: translateX(300px)
    → translateY(135px) scale(1,1) rotate(360deg);
```

```
        transform: translateX(300px)
     → translateY(135px) scale(1,1)
     → rotate(360deg);
}


50% {

-webkit-transform: translateX(400px)
 → translateY(270px) scale(1,1) rotate(90deg);

   -ms-transform: translateX(400px)
    → translateY(270px) scale(1,1) rotate(90deg);

        transform: translateX(400px)
     → translateY(270px) scale(1,1)
     → rotate(90deg);
}


53% {

-webkit-transform: translateX(480px)
 → translateY(370px) scale(1,1) rotate(180deg);

   -ms-transform: translateX(480px)
    → translateY(370px) scale(1,1) rotate(180deg);

        transform: translateX(480px)
     → translateY(370px) scale(1,1)
     → rotate(180deg);
}


55% {

-webkit-transform: translateX(500px)
 → translateY(410px) scale(1.2,0.8) rotate(180deg);

   -ms-transform: translateX(500px)
    → translateY(410px) scale(1.2,0.8)
    → rotate(180deg);

        transform: translateX(500px)
     → translateY(410px) scale(1.2,0.8)
     → rotate(180deg);
}
```

```
58% {

-webkit-transform: translateX(520px)
→ translateY(370px) scale(0.9,1.1) rotate(180deg);

    -ms-transform: translateX(520px)
    → translateY(370px) scale(0.9,1.1)
    → rotate(180deg);

        transform: translateX(520px)
        → translateY(370px) scale(0.9,1.1)
        → rotate(180deg);

}


60% {

-webkit-transform: translateX(600px)
→ translateY(338px) scale(1,1) rotate(270deg);

    -ms-transform: translateX(600px)
    → translateY(338px) scale(1,1) rotate(270deg);

        transform: translateX(600px)
        → translateY(338px) scale(1,1)
        → rotate(270deg);

}


65% {

-webkit-transform: translateX(700px)
→ translateY(270px) scale(1,1) rotate(360deg);

    -ms-transform: translateX(700px)
    → translateY(270px) scale(1,1) rotate(360deg);

        transform: translateX(700px)
        → translateY(270px) scale(1,1)
        → rotate(360deg);

}


68% {

-webkit-transform: translateX(760px)
→ translateY(311px) scale(1,1) rotate(54deg);

    -ms-transform: translateX(760px)
    → translateY(311px) scale(1,1) rotate(54deg);
```

```
        transform: translateX(760px)
        ⟶ translateY(311px) scale(1,1)
        ⟶ rotate(54deg);
}


70% {

-webkit-transform: translateX(805px)
⟶ translateY(338px) scale(0.9,1.1) rotate(90deg);

    -ms-transform: translateX(805px)
    ⟶ translateY(338px) scale(0.9,1.1)
    ⟶ rotate(90deg);

        transform: translateX(805px)
        ⟶ translateY(338px) scale(0.9,1.1)
        ⟶ rotate(90deg);
}


72% {

-webkit-transform: translateX(760px)
⟶ translateY(311px) scale(1.05,0.95) rotate(36deg);

    -ms-transform: translateX(760px)
    ⟶ translateY(311px) scale(1.05,0.95)
    ⟶ rotate(36deg);

        transform: translateX(760px)
        ⟶ translateY(311px) scale(1.05,0.95)
        ⟶ rotate(36deg);
}


75% {

-webkit-transform: translateX(700px)
⟶ translateY(405px) scale(1,1) rotate(0deg);

    -ms-transform: translateX(700px)
    ⟶ translateY(405px) scale(1,1) rotate(0deg);

        transform: translateX(700px)
        ⟶ translateY(405px) scale(1,1) rotate(0deg);
}
```

```
80% {

-webkit-transform: translateX(650px)
⤳ translateY(371px) scale(1,1) rotate(-90deg);

    -ms-transform: translateX(650px)
    ⤳ translateY(371px) scale(1,1) rotate(-90deg);

        transform: translateX(650px)
        ⤳ translateY(371px) scale(1,1)
        ⤳ rotate(-90deg);

}


85% {

-webkit-transform: translateX(600px)
⤳ translateY(405px) scale(1,1) rotate(-180deg);

    -ms-transform: translateX(600px)
    ⤳ translateY(405px) scale(1,1) rotate(-180deg);

        transform: translateX(600px)
        ⤳ translateY(405px) scale(1,1)
        ⤳ rotate(-180deg);

}


90% {

-webkit-transform: translateX(525px)
⤳ translateY(405px) scale(1,1) rotate(-315deg);

    -ms-transform: translateX(525px)
    ⤳ translateY(405px) scale(1,1) rotate(-315deg);

        transform: translateX(525px)
        ⤳ translateY(405px) scale(1,1)
        rotate(-315deg);

}


95% {

-webkit-transform: translateX(450px)
⤳ translateY(405px) scale(1,1) rotate(-450deg);

    -ms-transform: translateX(450px)
    ⤳ translateY(405px) scale(1,1) rotate(-450deg);
```

```
                    transform: translateX(450px)
                  ↪ translateY(405px) scale(1,1)
                  ↪ rotate(-450deg);

        }


        99% {

        -webkit-transform: translateX(365px)
          ↪ translateY(400px) scale(0.8,1.2) rotate(-585deg);

            -ms-transform: translateX(365px)
              ↪ translateY(400px) scale(0.8,1.2)
              ↪ rotate(-585deg);

                    transform: translateX(365px)
                  ↪ translateY(400px) scale(0.8,1.2)
                  ↪ rotate(-585deg);

        }


        100% {

        -webkit-transform: translateX(375px)
          ↪ translateY(405px) scale(1,1) rotate(-570deg);

            -ms-transform: translateX(375px)
              ↪ translateY(405px) scale(1,1) rotate(-570deg);

                    transform: translateX(375px)
                  ↪ translateY(405px) scale(1,1)
                  ↪ rotate(-570deg);

        }


    }
```

There's a lot going on in these 25 keyframes. Four transformations are at work: translation in the x- and y-axes, scaling, and rotation. Varying the distance the ball travels in each axis from keyframe to keyframe creates something of an arc.

Scaling is used sparingly when the ball makes contact with another object and deforms. To help the realism, I set the ball to rotate in the direction of its motion, which can be considered overlapping action.

5. Reload the page to watch the complete animation (**FIGURE 5.7**).

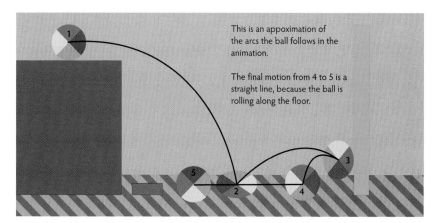

This is an appoximation of the arcs the ball follows in the animation.

The final motion from 4 to 5 is a straight line, because the ball is rolling along the floor.

FIGURE 5.7
Arcs

The first 30 percent worth of keyframes is the anticipation. The ball rolls back toward the edge of the stage, makes contact with it, and squashes itself before rolling back to its starting point. From there it rolls off the table and bounces on the floor before bouncing against the wall. After making contact with the wall, the ball bounces back in the opposite direction, changes the direction of its rotation, and rolls along the floor until it comes to rest against the stopper.

The first bounce is the main action; the follow-through is the bounce against the wall and everything after. At each point where the ball bounces, you've added a slight squash and stretch deformation. You added keyframes near the deformation to slow down the action for a moment.

As amateurish as the animation is now, it's magnitudes more realistic than where you started.

Secondary Action

Objects in the real world don't wait for other objects to start before starting their motion. Additional motion from other objects or parts of objects adds life and realism to an animation.

Overlapping actions don't wait—secondary actions don't either. Secondary actions are similar to overlapping actions in the sense that they're minor compared to the main action in the scene. They differ in that they occur independently of the main action, not as a result of the main action.

For example, say you're animating an alien from another planet. This alien has antenna. The antenna might be moving around at all times regardless of whether the space alien is moving in any other way. Perhaps as the alien walks the antenna are moving about sensing the environment. Because the antenna action is independent of the main action, it's considered secondary action.

If the alien's antenna were moving only as a result of the main action (swinging back and forth after the alien ran and stopped, for example), the antenna action would be considered follow-through or overlapping action instead.

To be honest, it can be a bit confusing and difficult to decide how dependent one action is on another. Don't worry too much about it. The name itself is less important than having the secondary or overlapping actions occurring in addition to the main action.

Secondary actions should support and emphasize the main action and not compete with it. They are secondary and not primary actions, after all. If the main action is especially dramatic, you might want to place secondary actions at the start and end and let the main action dominate the rest of the animation. More common, though, is for secondary actions to be subtle. They should be felt instead of directly noticed, reinforcing the mood and atmosphere.

In the previous example, the rotation of the ball might be seen as secondary action. I think I'd call it overlapping action as the rotation (rolling) of the ball is part of the main action of moving and bouncing across the stage. Making the distinction between the two can be difficult.

Timing

As you would expect, timing is critical in animation. The speed and acceleration of objects gives a sense of what the object is, its weight, its size, and why it's moving.

Think about the blink of an eye. A fast blink can suggest a character is alert. A slow blink might suggest the character is tired or sluggish. The timing alone is enough to communicate different impressions.

Timing can help communicate the characters' emotional state. It can help communicate the mood and atmosphere of the animation. It can add personality to objects and characters. If you handle timing well, the objects in your animation will appear to obey the laws of physics. Get the timing wrong and something will feel wrong.

An object's size and weight can suggest how fast it might move in general and in reaction to being pushed or pulled. Large, heavy objects will naturally move slower than smaller, light objects. Have a small object dart quickly around a slow, large object and the juxtapositions of big and small, fast and slow can generate all sorts of emotive power.

You've been working with timing throughout this chapter—most noticeably when you added keyframes for anticipation, follow-through, or entering and exiting a bounce. When exploring the different values that I ultimately used to create these animations, many of the changes were to improve the timing of everything.

When the timing isn't right, the animation won't appear smooth and instead will have some choppy moments where the timing for one keyframe doesn't flow naturally into the timing of the keyframes before and after.

Exaggeration

This might sound strange, but if your animation tried to imitate reality perfectly, it could end up appearing static and lifeless. Some exaggeration can make the animation appear more realistic. In fact, animated characters require some exaggeration for realism.

Exaggeration accents actions and emotions. You might have an arm swing too far forward and back to call attention to the swing. You can exaggerate important poses and motions to emphasize them. Facial expressions are often exaggerated in animation. Think of cartoon characters' eyes flying out of their head when startled.

You should be careful when using exaggeration. Don't exaggerate everything. Use restraint and balance in what you do and don't exaggerate. It's not something you want to use arbitrarily.

You exaggerate something to give it a little more life and excitement, but not so much that you completely destroy believability. Keep in mind that the rules of believability are established by the animation. No one's eyes pop out when startled, but it's perfectly acceptable and even expected in the cartoon world.

Disney tries to stay true to reality—exaggerated animation is simply reality, but a bit more extreme. How much you choose to use it can depend on your style as well as the specifics of the animation.

Exaggeration can also involve the supernatural or surreal. It can alter the features of a character or object. It can even alter the storyline of the animation. Remember that restraint is important: Some exaggeration helps the realism; too much takes away from it.

A lot of people consider exaggeration the most fun part of animation and the most entertaining of the 12 principles. Animation without any exaggeration can feel stiff and mechanical no matter how realistically accurate. Exaggerate a few parts of the animation and it becomes more dynamic and exciting. It comes alive.

Exaggeration doesn't necessarily mean extreme distortion. Any exaggeration you add should reinforce the main action and overall animation. See it as a way to add an additional layer of drama and excitement.

1. Add some exaggeration to the rolling and bouncing animation by increasing the squashing of the ball (**EXAMPLE 5.8**). The only changes you need to make are to some of the scaling values. Once again, in the interest of saving space, I'll show only the non-vendor-prefixed **@keyframes** rule. Don't forget to add the **@-webkit-keyframes** version.

```
@keyframes bounce {

    0% {
    -webkit-transform: translateX(0) translateY(0px)
     → scale(1,1) rotate(90deg);
        -ms-transform: translateX(0) translateY(0px)
         → scale(1,1) rotate(90deg);
            transform: translateX(0) translateY(0px)
             → scale(1,1) rotate(90deg);
    }

    15% {
    -webkit-transform: translateX(-100px) translateY(0px)
     → scale(1,1) rotate(-90deg);
```

```
      -ms-transform: translateX(-100px) translateY(0px)
   ⟶ scale(1,1) rotate(-90deg);

         transform: translateX(-100px) translateY(0px)
         ⟶ scale(1,1) rotate(-90deg);
}


25% {

-webkit-transform: translateX(-120px)
⟶ translateY(-30px) scale(0.4,1.6) rotate(-90deg);

   -ms-transform: translateX(-120px)
   ⟶ translateY(-30px) scale(0.4,1.6)
   ⟶ rotate(-90deg);

      transform: translateX(-120px)
      ⟶ translateY(-30px) scale(0.4,1.6)
      ⟶ rotate(-90deg);
}


27% {

-webkit-transform: translateX(-120px)
⟶ translateY(-30px) scale(0.4,1.6) rotate(-90deg);

   -ms-transform: translateX(-120px)
   ⟶ translateY(-30px) scale(0.4,1.6)
   ⟶ rotate(-90deg);

      transform: translateX(-120px)
      ⟶ translateY(-30px) scale(0.4,1.6)
      ⟶ rotate(-90deg);
}


28% {

-webkit-transform: translateX(-100px) translateY(0px)
⟶ scale(1,1) rotate(-75deg);

   -ms-transform: translateX(-100px) translateY(0px)
   ⟶ scale(1,1) rotate(-75deg);

      transform: translateX(-100px) translateY(0px)
      ⟶ scale(1,1) rotate(-75deg);
}
```

```
31% {

-webkit-transform: translateX(0px) translateY(0px)
→ scale(1,1) rotate(90deg);

    -ms-transform: translateX(0px) translateY(0px)
    → scale(1,1) rotate(90deg);

        transform: translateX(0px) translateY(0px)
        → scale(1,1) rotate(90deg);

}


35% {

-webkit-transform: translateX(100px) translateY(0px)
→ scale(1,1) rotate(180deg);

    -ms-transform: translateX(100px) translateY(0px)
    → scale(1,1) rotate(180deg);

        transform: translateX(100px) translateY(0px)
        → scale(1,1) rotate(180deg);

}

40% {

-webkit-transform: translateX(200px) translateY(0px)
→ scale(1,1) rotate(270deg);

    -ms-transform: translateX(200px) translateY(0px)
    → scale(1,1) rotate(270deg);

        transform: translateX(200px) translateY(0px)
        → scale(1,1) rotate(270deg);

}

45% {

-webkit-transform: translateX(300px)
→ translateY(135px) scale(1,1) rotate(360deg);

    -ms-transform: translateX(300px)
    → translateY(135px) scale(1,1) rotate(360deg);
```

```
        transform: translateX(300px)
    →  translateY(135px) scale(1,1)
    →  rotate(360deg);
}


50% {

-webkit-transform: translateX(400px)
→  translateY(270px) scale(1,1) rotate(90deg);

    -ms-transform: translateX(400px)
    →  translateY(270px) scale(1,1) rotate(90deg);

        transform: translateX(400px)
    →  translateY(270px) scale(1,1)
    →  rotate(90deg);
}


53% {

-webkit-transform: translateX(480px)
→  translateY(370px) scale(1,1) rotate(180deg);

    -ms-transform: translateX(480px)
    →  translateY(370px) scale(1,1) rotate(180deg);

        transform: translateX(480px)
    →  translateY(370px) scale(1,1)
    →  rotate(180deg);
}


55% {

-webkit-transform: translateX(500px)
→  translateY(430px) scale(1.5,0.5) rotate(180deg);

    -ms-transform: translateX(500px)
    →  translateY(430px) scale(1.5,0.5)
    →  rotate(180deg);

        transform: translateX(500px)
    →  translateY(430px) scale(1.5,0.5)
    →  rotate(180deg);
}
```

```
58% {

-webkit-transform: translateX(520px)
→ translateY(370px) scale(0.9,1.1) rotate(180deg);

   -ms-transform: translateX(520px)
    → translateY(370px) scale(0.9,1.1)
    → rotate(180deg);

      transform: translateX(520px)
       → translateY(370px) scale(0.9,1.1)
       → rotate(180deg);

}


60% {

-webkit-transform: translateX(600px)
→ translateY(338px) scale(1,1) rotate(270deg);

   -ms-transform: translateX(600px)
    → translateY(338px) scale(1,1) rotate(270deg);

      transform: translateX(600px)
       → translateY(338px) scale(1,1)
       → rotate(270deg);

}


65% {

-webkit-transform: translateX(700px)
→ translateY(270px) scale(1,1) rotate(360deg);

   -ms-transform: translateX(700px)
    → translateY(270px) scale(1,1) rotate(360deg);

      transform: translateX(700px)
       → translateY(270px) scale(1,1)
       → rotate(360deg);

}


68% {

-webkit-transform: translateX(760px)
→ translateY(311px) scale(1,1) rotate(54deg);

   -ms-transform: translateX(760px)
    → translateY(311px) scale(1,1) rotate(54deg);
```

```
        transform: translateX(760px)
    →  translateY(311px) scale(1,1)
    →  rotate(54deg);

}


70% {

-webkit-transform: translateX(820px)
→ translateY(338px) scale(0.8,1.2) rotate(90deg);

    -ms-transform: translateX(820px)
    →  translateY(338px) scale(0.8,1.2)
    →  rotate(90deg);

        transform: translateX(820px)
        →  translateY(338px) scale(0.8,1.2)
        →  rotate(90deg);

}


72% {

-webkit-transform: translateX(760px)
→ translateY(311px) scale(1.05,0.95) rotate(36deg);

    -ms-transform: translateX(760px)
    →  translateY(311px) scale(1.05,0.95)
    →  rotate(36deg);

        transform: translateX(760px)
        →  translateY(311px) scale(1.05,0.95)
        →  rotate(36deg);

}


75% {

-webkit-transform: translateX(700px)
→ translateY(405px) scale(1,1) rotate(0deg);

    -ms-transform: translateX(700px)
    →  translateY(405px) scale(1,1) rotate(0deg);

        transform: translateX(700px)
        →  translateY(405px) scale(1,1) rotate(0deg);

}
```

```
80% {

-webkit-transform: translateX(650px)
→ translateY(371px) scale(1,1) rotate(-90deg);

    -ms-transform: translateX(650px)
    → translateY(371px) scale(1,1) rotate(-90deg);

        transform: translateX(650px)
        → translateY(371px) scale(1,1)
        → rotate(-90deg);

}


85% {

-webkit-transform: translateX(600px)
→ translateY(405px) scale(1,1) rotate(-180deg);

    -ms-transform: translateX(600px)
    → translateY(405px) scale(1,1) rotate(-180deg);

        transform: translateX(600px)
        → translateY(405px) scale(1,1)
        → rotate(-180deg);

}


90% {

-webkit-transform: translateX(525px)
→ translateY(405px) scale(1,1) rotate(-315deg);

    -ms-transform: translateX(525px)
    → translateY(405px) scale(1,1) rotate(-315deg);

        transform: translateX(525px)
        → translateY(405px) scale(1,1)
        → rotate(-315deg);

}


95% {

-webkit-transform: translateX(450px)
→ translateY(405px) scale(1,1) rotate(-450deg);
```

```
    -ms-transform: translateX(450px)
  → translateY(405px) scale(1,1) rotate(-450deg);

      transform: translateX(450px)
    → translateY(405px) scale(1,1)
    → rotate(-450deg);

}


99% {

-webkit-transform: translateX(360px)
→ translateY(400px) scale(0.7,1.3) rotate(-585deg);

    -ms-transform: translateX(360px)
  → translateY(400px) scale(0.7,1.3)
  → rotate(-585deg);

      transform: translateX(360px)
    → translateY(400px) scale(0.7,1.3)
    → rotate(-585deg);

}


100% {

-webkit-transform: translateX(375px)
→ translateY(405px) scale(1,1) rotate(-570deg);

    -ms-transform: translateX(375px)
  → translateY(405px) scale(1,1) rotate(-570deg);

      transform: translateX(375px)
    → translateY(405px) scale(1,1)
    → rotate(-570deg);

}


}
```

2. Reload the page with the now more exaggerated squashing and compare it
   to the animation without the exaggeration.

FIGURE 5.8 isolates parts of the animation where the ball deforms and com-
pares the original deformation from the previous @keyframes rule with the
exaggerated deformation from this one.

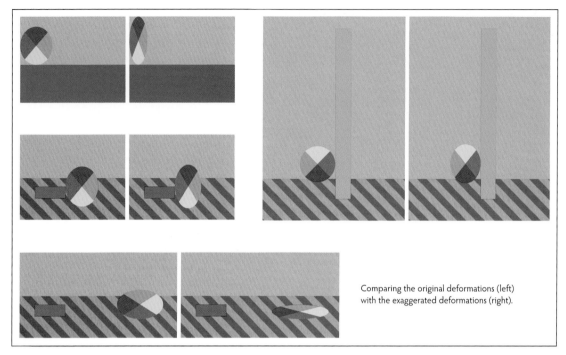

Comparing the original deformations (left) with the exaggerated deformations (right).

FIGURE 5.8
Exaggeration

Solid Drawing

The solid drawing principle takes into account 3-dimensional space and gives mass and weight to the animated objects, staying true to the 3-dimensionality of the real world as we perceive it. We don't expect much movement from 2-dimensional objects, so making them appear solid also makes them appear to have the potential for movement.

The responsibility for this principle is for the animators who are drawing the characters and objects. It's a reminder that even in the age of computers, drawing is a valuable skill. An animator should be able to draw believable figures and objects from any side and any angle. Drawing them as though they're in 3-dimensional space creates the illusion of life.

Most website animation won't involve complex characters and objects. The current trend is for a generally flat aesthetic. Still there are things you can do to create 3-dimensional space without drawing, even during this flat trend.

You can add slight and reserved shadows and gradients to objects. You can play with scale to create perspective and foreshortening. You can add pattern and texture to give objects mass and volume. Anything you do to give a sense of depth and 3-dimensionality to an animation falls under this principle.

Solid drawing are what we typically think of as animation with characters and a story. You'll be less concerned with it when it comes to designing interface objects, but you'll still have some concern.

The animation you've been working with doesn't have a lot of solid drawing, although it does include the floor pattern, which creates a sense of 3-dimensional space. You could add a shadow that follows the ball around and have it grow and shrink depending on where the light source is in relation to the ball. You might use borders or shadows on the table, wall, and stopper to give them more mass. You might use gradients to mimic the play of light over the surface of any object.

Appeal

The last of the 12 principles is appeal, and it's similar to the charisma of a real person. Appeal is that "it" factor that makes us think a character is something more than just a character in an animation. Appeal isn't only for likable and sympathetic characters. Villains can have appeal—sometimes they have more appeal than the heroes in the story.

Animation viewers should find the character or object interesting or, even better, captivating. This can mean making the character be anything the viewer would like that character to be. Most characters won't be appealing to everyone, no matter how much appeal some think they have.

Simplicity helps create appeal. Complexity tends to lack appeal. Symmetry and a baby-like face can often effectively add appeal for likable characters, although not so much for villainous characters.

Try not to be weak when creating appealing characters. Be bold. Make characters and objects larger than life. Your goal is to bring your animated characters to life and make them something more than animation. Give them emotion and let them communicate that emotion to the viewer.

Create characters that are different from one another, acting differently and with different emotional states. Give each character or object a distinct personality that's familiar to the audience. Give them unique mannerisms and traits.

In the end, the appeal of the characters and objects in your animation will ultimately be what determines success.

Beyond the 12 Principles

In 2009, another Disney animator and animation trainer published *Drawn to Life: 20 Golden Years of Disney Master Classes: Volume 1: The Walt Stanchfield Lectures*. A similarly titled volume 2 was published around the same time. Inside the two volumes are 28 principles of animation:

* www.amazon.com/Drawn-Life-Classes-Stanchfield-Lectures/dp/0240810961

* www.amazon.com/Drawn-Life-Classes-Stanchfield-Lectures/dp/0240811070

Some of the 28 principles will be familiar to you after reading this chapter. Many of them look like subprinciples of the first 12. You and I are probably fine with 12 principles to guide us in interface design, but the more interested and adventuresome of us might be interested in the rest.

* Pose and mood
* Shape and form
* Anatomy
* Model or character
* Weight
* Line and silhouette
* Action and reaction
* Perspective
* Direction
* Tension
* Planes

* Solidity
* Arcs
* Squash and stretch
* Beat and rhythm
* Depth and volume
* Overlap and follow-through
* Timing
* Working from extreme to extreme
* Straights and curves
* Primary and secondary action
* Staging and composition

- Anticipation
- Caricature
- Details
- Texture
- Simplification
- Positive and negative shapes

Closing Thoughts

Disney's 12 principles of animation evolved out of a desire to create more realistic animations. Most of the work you do as a web designer isn't about creating appealing characters performing exaggerated actions. Perhaps you have an interest in creating animated stories that do, but I assume most of you are more interested in the kind of animation that enhances user interfaces (UI).

Even if enhancing UIs is your only goal, these principles are useful. Many animations you encounter on websites and most definitely the better ones, will exhibit one or more of these principles. For example, the rubber-band effect when you scroll to the end of something shows follow-through and exaggeration. Slide to unlock on the iPhone is an example of anticipation. Almost everything you do as a designer involves staging in some way.

Animations of interface elements establish connections between the before and after states. Imagine a thumbnail opening a pop-up with a larger version of the image when clicked. Without the animation, a viewer might not instantly get the connection that the large image is the same one as in the thumbnail. It might appear to be a new image that appeared instantly on top of the first one.

Remember not to overdo it. Show some restraint and use animation sparingly and subtly. Save it for the most important changes that occur. You don't need to bring every property change to life through animation. You never want animation to get in the way of a site's functionality, and too much animation can and probably will get in the way and distract from your main message. It can become annoying to have to wait even a second or two when that wait always precedes something you want to do and is showing you something you've seen dozens or hundreds of times before.

Designers animate to focus attention on certain areas, to engage more with an audience, and to add delight and appeal to a site. You can do all these things better by following the 12 principles and creating more realistic animation.

You can also go beyond the 12 principles and take it upon yourself to observe nature and objects in the real world. Pay attention to their motion. How do they start? How do they stop? How do they move in between? Pay attention not only to the creatures and objects in the world, but also to the laws of physics under which they operate. That's how all these principles came about in the first place.

The principles were developed specifically for story animation, but we can use them when animating a website interface. The next chapter presents a variety of more practical animation examples that you can use on the next website you create.

CHAPTER 6

EXAMPLES

At the beginning of this book, I mentioned that the recent trend in web design is to remove the depth of skeuomorphism in favor of a flat aesthetic. That's fine. Trends come and go and will come and go again. Today's flat design is tomorrow's next trend.

One unfortunate result of removing the realistic depth cues is a perceptual loss of physical space and a loss of some of the details that delight visitors. Motion can step in to return some of both.

Animation can help establish physical space by showing how objects move about within the page. Where are the boundaries they bump into? Do some overlap others? Do they appear to move in and out of the screen? Motion can offer some context for how to answer these and similar questions.

The examples in this book have all been simple and abstract, so I wanted to leave you with a few examples that are more practical. I'll walk you through four examples in this chapter.

- A simple navigation bar with a drop-down menu
- Modal windows that open when clicking an element
- Off-canvas sidebar navigation that slides in and out of the page
- A content switcher, similar to an image slider

How to Use the Examples

So far the examples in this book have not been anything you'd use in the design of a real website. I've kept things simple and abstract to make learning the principles easier. Even the bouncing ball from the previous chapter is semi-realistic at best. Any lack of realism was a result of my animation skills.

Fortunately, the kind of animation where my skills are lacking—the kind of animation you think of when you think of Disney—isn't the kind of animation you'll typically add to a website. You might use that kind of animation, depending on the site, but the majority of us won't ever animate characters and stories.

Most of us are looking to enhance the communication in a design or simply add some delight. This chapter presents some practical examples where adding transitions and animations to your design elements communicates something more or simply creates some positive emotional appeal—one of the 12 principles, by the way.

Use your imagination as you work through the examples. I didn't place anything inside the content switcher example, but you can. Think about what you can put into the content switcher, or think about the technique used to make the switch and where else you can apply it. Please play with the code. Modify the values. Expand on what each example does. Hopefully, you'll find the code useful for your own projects.

The examples that follow are just a few of the many ways you can animate your design elements. They aren't the only ways.

The live examples use the following code at the top of the CSS, but for space reasons, it isn't included in the example code I'm showing in this chapter.

```
* {
    box-sizing: border-box;
}

body {
    font-family: "helvetica", "sans-serif";
```

```
    font-size: 100%;

    margin: 0;

    padding: 0;

}
```

If you've never seen the **box-sizing** property before, do a quick online search. It's a great property that you'll likely want to use in every project. Normally, the box model considers the width you set to be equal to the width of the content box + the width of the padding + the width of the border. This means that changing either the padding or border thickness requires you to change your width too, if you want to keep the overall width of your element the same.

With **box-sizing** set to **border-box** you don't have to worry about it. When you set a width, it's the width of the overall element and not the width of the content box. This is probably how you think about it anyway. It's not necessary, but it makes things much easier. I've also used it throughout the examples, so if you don't include it, some elements won't align as they should.

Just remember to include * { **box-sizing: border-box;** } at the top of every example.

The styles on the **body** are just to set a font and size and to zero out padding and margin.

How about some practical examples?

Navigation Bar

Let's start with an example of something I'm sure you've developed many times: a navigation bar. I'm guessing you've built at least one or two navbars before. Now you're going to build the one in **FIGURE 6.1** (**EXAMPLE 6.1**).

FIGURE 6.1
Navigation bar

1. Create an unordered list of links in your HTML.

```
<ul class="menu">
    <li><a href="">Item 1</a></li>
    <li><a href="">Item 2</a></li>
    <li><a href="">Item 3</a></li>
    <li><a href="">Item 4</a></li>
    <li><a href="">Item 5</a></li>
</ul>
```

This pattern is rather standard when developing a list of links for a menu. This code uses a class of menu, but otherwise it's an ordinary list of links. The menu items won't actually do anything; the code doesn't use real links, but that's OK for the purpose of the example.

2. Add the following CSS to turn the list of links into a horizontal navigation bar:

```
.menu {
    list-style: none;
    padding: 0;
    margin: 0;
    width: 100%;
    background: #555;
    text-align: center;
    position: relative;
    z-index: 0;

    display: table;          /* fix for Safari */
}

.menu > li {
    display: inline-block;
    zoom: 1;                 /* fix for IE7 and IE6
    _display: inline;        /* fix for IE7 and IE6 */
}
```

```
.menu a {

    text-decoration: none;

    display: block;

    padding: 0.75em 1.5em;

    background: #555;

    color: #fff;

}


.menu a:hover {

    background: #777;

}
```

A few things are going on in this code. First you reset the default `margin` and `padding` on the unordered list (`.menu`) and remove the default bullets as well. You also remove the underline on the links (`.menu a`) by setting `text-decoration: none`.

By default, list items display as block-level elements (vertically on top of each other). But you want the list items to appear horizontally. This is going to be a horizontal navigation bar. There are a few ways you can do this:

◆ Floating the list items

◆ Setting the list items to display as inline-block elements

◆ Setting the whole list as a CSS table

The first is the most common way to set up horizontal navigation in a list, but this example code uses the `inline-block` method. The choice to use the `inline-block` method was in part to show you something different and in part to make it easy to center the menu items. The latter requires a little more work using floats than `text-align: center`.

Note the selector for the list items. It is the direct child selector `.menu > li`. Later in this example, you'll add a drop-down menu, which will display vertically. You don't want those list items to display as inline blocks, so by using the direct child selector, you target only the direct list items of the `.menu` list and not any list items in the submenu that you'll add later.

Notice the comments in the code that identify the fixes for various browsers. Older versions of IE don't support `inline-block`. Adding `zoom: 1` is a fix that tells IE6 and IE7 to view list items as block-level elements, whereas `_display: inline` is a fix to make them display as inline elements. This effectively lets you turn the list items into inline-blocks in IE6 and IE7, even though neither supports `inline-block`.

The latter fix uses an old hack known as the underscore hack—asterisks (*) and other characters also work. Older versions of IE ignore the underscore and see `_display` as `display`. All other brothers and newer versions of IE ignore it completely. The hack was a way to target IE only—before people were using conditional comments to do the same.

There's also a fix on the `.menu` class for a different issue. Setting `display` as `inline-block` brings with it an issue of extra space between elements. The extra space is 0.25em wide. There are a handful of ways (none perfect) to get browsers to remove the space.

The example uses the `display: table` method as a fix. Other fixes are to set the `word-spacing` to `-0.25em` to close the space or simply remove the whitespace in your HTML.

In the example, you change the links (`.menu a`) to display as block-level elements instead of their default inline. The reason is so that the links will fill their container. That means visitors can hover over and click the entire list item and not just the text.

The rest of the code is for aesthetics. You set a background color on the menu and the links. You add some padding to the links to give the text some room to breathe. And you change the text color to white so it can be read against the dark gray background.

Finally, you set the links to change to a lighter gray on hover.

3. Load the file in a browser.

A medium gray bar displays across the top of the page. In the center are five links named Item 1 through Item 5. Hovering over any of these changes the background color to a lighter shade of gray.

Pretty standard stuff.

There's only one change occurring—the change in background color when you hover over a link. If you're going to animate anything here, that would be it.

> **TIP**
>
> If for some reason my fix doesn't work in your browser, there are other options for correcting the extra space. I wrote an article about the different options, which you can find at www.vanseodesign.com/css/inline-blocks.

4. Create a transition for the change in background color on the link with the following code. Add it to your CSS for links inside the `.menu` class. Changes in the code are highlighted.

```
.menu a {
    display: block;
    padding: 0.75em 1.5em;
    background: #555;
    text-decoration: none;
    color: #fff;

    -webkit-transition: background 0.5s;
            transition: background 0.5s;
}
```

It's a very subtle change, but you can feel it. If you aren't sure that the transition is working, change the timing to something longer than 0.5 seconds. Change it to 5 seconds or 10 seconds so you know the transition is occurring, and then change it to something that looks good to you. Feel free to experiment with different times. Even 0.5 seconds makes a difference from the abrupt, instant change without a transition.

Even in browsers that don't support transitions, the change in color still works. The transition improves the experience, but it isn't a requirement to make things work.

You might be wondering why use a transition and not an animation. It's a good question, and you can certainly set this up using keyframes. However, because it's a very simple change and because you want it to trigger only on hover, a transition seems like the better choice. You'll likely find yourself using transitions more often than animations.

You might also ask why transition the background color. Isn't that one of the properties that could have performance issues? Yes, it could. Remember, anything other than transforms and opacity could result in a performance hit. However, background color is such a useful change to transition or animate that you should be willing to take the risk.

Let's extend the navigation bar and give it a drop-down menu (**FIGURE 6.2**).

FIGURE 6.2
Navigation bar with drop-
down menu

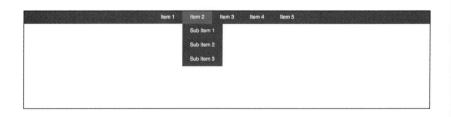

5. Replace your HTML with the following HTML:

```
<ul class="menu">
    <li><a href="">Item 1</a></li>
    <li><a href="">Item 2</a>
        <ul class="submenu">
            <li><a href="">Sub Item 1</a></li>
            <li><a href="">Sub Item 2</a></li>
            <li><a href="">Sub Item 3</a></li>
        </ul>
    </li>
    <li><a href="">Item 3</a></li>
    <li><a href="">Item 4</a></li>
    <li><a href="">Item 5</a></li>
</ul>
```

You've added another unordered list with a class of `submenu` inside the
Item 2 list item code. It has three subitems, and you'll make it drop down
from the top-level Item 2.

6. Style the submenu with the following CSS:

```
.submenu {

    list-style: none;
    padding: 0;
    margin: 0
    text-align: left;
```

```
        background: #555;

        position: absolute;

}


.submenu a {

        padding: 0.75em 1.5em;

        border-bottom: 1px solid #666;

}
```

First, you reset the `list-style`, `padding`, and `margin`. Then you switch the text to display aligned `left` and give the `.submenu` a `background` color. The link gets some `padding` and a `border-bottom`. You might wonder why the need for positioning. By default, the `.submenu` is in the normal document flow and will break the layout of the top-level menu. Setting it to `position: absolute` removes it from the document flow and allows the top level of the menu to display properly.

If you were to load everything in a browser now, the submenu would be visible. That's not what you want. You want it to be hidden until someone hovers over the Item 2 link. There are several ways to do that. The most common is to position the submenu somewhere off the page and reposition it when hovering over the link.

Let's try something different.

7. Set up the functionality on the drop-down list. Changes in the code are highlighted.

```
.submenu {

        list-style: none;

        padding: 0;

        text-align: left;

        background: #555;

        position: absolute;

        opacity: 0;

}
```

```
.menu li:hover .submenu {

    opacity: 1.0;

}
```

To hide the `.submenu`, you set its `opacity` to `0`. Then you set it back to `1` when someone hovers over the list item that's the parent for the `.submenu`.

8. Reload the page. The menu and submenu work properly.

   However, the submenu appears instantly and abruptly when hovering over the list item. You correct this in the next step.

9. Add a transition to the `.submenu`. Changes in the code are highlighted.

```
.submenu {

    list-style: none;
    padding: 0;
    text-align: left;
    background: #555;
    position: absolute;
    z-index: -1;
    opacity: 0;

    -webkit-transition: opacity 0.75s ease 0.01s;
            transition: opacity 0.75s ease 0.01s;

}
```

You added a simple transition for changes in opacity. It has an ever so slight delay time of 0.01 second, which makes everything a little smoother.

10. Reload your page again, and check the transitions.

    Both the change in background color on the top-level menu items and the change in transition on the `.submenu` are subtle, but effective.

11. Remove the two transitions you added in steps 4 and 9, and compare to see the difference.

Let's try something else. Instead of hiding and showing the `.submenu` using `opacity`, let's use the more common technique of moving it off the page and bringing it back.

12. Replace your CSS for the submenu with the following. Additions and changes in the code are highlighted.

```css
.submenu {

    list-style: none;

    padding: 0;

    text-align: left;

    background: #555;

    position: absolute;

    z-index: -1;

    -webkit-transform: translateY(-10em);

            transform: translateY(-10em);

    -webkit-transition: -webkit-transform 0.75s
 →  ease 0.01s;

            transition: transform 0.75s ease 0.01s;

}

.submenu a {

    padding: 0.75em 1.5em;

    border-bottom: 1px solid #666;

}

.menu li:hover .submenu {

    -webkit-transform: translateY(0);

            transform: translateY(0);

}
```

To position the `.submenu` off the page initially, you use the `translateY()` function. Using `-10em` works to move the `.submenu` enough to hide it completely. On hover, you reset the `translateY()` function to `0`. The transition is the same as before, except it now transitions over transformations instead of `opacity`.

The reason for setting `z-index: -1` is because otherwise the `.submenu` would slide in on top of `.menu`, which wouldn't look right. It's also why you added relative position and a `z-index` of `0` to the `.menu` class in step 2. Giving the submenu a negative `z-index` makes the `.submenu` appear to slide out from under the top-level menu.

13. Reload your page one more time, and observe the difference.

    Either approach (`opacity` or `transform`) works well to make the submenu appear less jarring. However, the transform-only approach has a problem.

    It relies on transforms to make it work. Any browser that doesn't support transforms won't ever display the drop-down list. That might be OK, if you provide alternate navigation to the items in the drop-down list. If the drop-down list is the only way to access those links, then you need to use a different solution. Fortunately, you aren't limited to using one method. The `opacity` change should work in all browsers, so let's add it back.

14. Add the `opacity` transition back to your CSS. Additions and changes in the code are highlighted.

    ```
    .submenu {

        list-style: none;
        padding: 0;
        text-align: left;
        background: #555;
        position: absolute;
        z-index: -1;

        opacity: 0;
    ```

```
        -webkit-transform: translateY(-10em);
                transform: translateY(-10em);

        -webkit-transition: opacity 0.75s ease 0.01s,
        ⇢ -webkit-transform 0.75s ease 0.01s;
                transition: opacity 0.75s ease 0.01s,
                ⇢ transform 0.75s ease 0.01s;

}

.submenu a {
    padding: 0.75em 1.5em;
    border-bottom: 1px solid #666;
}

.menu li:hover .submenu {
    opacity: 1.0;

    -webkit-transform: translateY(0);
            transform: translateY(0);
}
```

All you're doing with this code is adding back the **opacity** transition you removed in step 12.

15. Reload your page one last time, and see what you think about using both transitions.

Once again, as subtle as the transitions in this example might seem, they have a huge impact on anyone using the navigation bar. Without the transitions, the navbar works, but the changes feel abrupt. The transitions don't alter the functionality at all, but they do make all the changes feel smoother and more natural.

Ready for the next example?

Modal Windows

It's common to send people to a new page to have them log in or complete a contact form. At times it would be nice to let them fill in a form without having to visit a new page. Instead you might open a modal window that contains the form. Your visitors fill in their information, submit the form, and get back to what they were doing on the page.

There is some debate about whether or not you should ever use a modal window. Users have to interact with a modal window in some way before they can do anything else on the page. Because of this, some suggest it's a bad idea to use them. Others say modal windows should open things you likely want to focus on. For example, if you click a link or button to log in, it stands to reason you want to log in. If you were expecting a new page (the alternative), you would need at least one click to get back to what you were doing, which is the same as closing a modal window.

Debate aside, you'll create a modal window in this example. First, you'll create a button that when clicked opens a new window containing a login form (**FIGURE 6.3**). The form won't be a working form, but it'll look like a form with a Login button that does nothing and a Close button that closes the modal window.

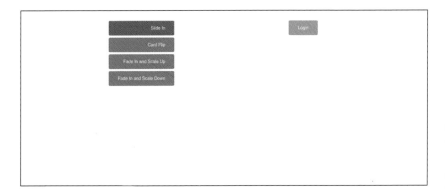

Once that's all set up, you'll add some transitions so the window opens (**FIGURE 6.4**) and closes smoothly.

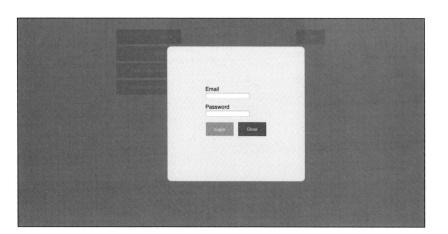

FIGURE 6.4
Modal window open

1. Add the following code to a new HTML file:

```
<div class="container" id="open">
    <div class="modal-container">
        <div class="modal">
            <form class="login">
                <label>Email</label>
                <input type="email" />

                <label>Password</label>
                <input type="password" />

                <input type="submit" value="Login" />
                <a href="#" class="close">Close</a>
            </form>
        </div>
    </div>
    <a href="#open" class="btn">Login</a>

    <div class="overlay"></div>
</div>
```

Let's take a look at what's going on in this code. It's easier to see from the inside out. You create a `form` with a class of `login`. Inside the `form` are labels and input fields for an email address and a password. There's also a `submit` button and a link with a class of `close`. Note the link points to a hash mark as a URL. This is part of how you open and close the modal window.

The entire form is wrapped in a `div` with a class of `modal`. In addition to the form that's inside the `.modal div`, there's a link that will become another Login button. This is the one that you'll click to open the modal window. In addition to a class of `.btn` on the link, you're setting the `href` attribute to `#open`. That loads the URL of the current page with `#open` appended, like a named anchor. You'll use this named anchor to open and close the modal window.

Below the `.btn` link, there's a `div` with a class of `overlay`. This `div` displays on top of everything except the modal window when it's open, effectively keeping you from clicking on anything not inside the modal window.

The `.modal` window is wrapped by a `.modal-container div`. This won't come into play until later in the example for one specific transitional effect, and you'll learn more about it in a moment.

Finally, everything is wrapped in a `.container div` that's also been given an `id` of `"open"`, to match the named anchor. You're going to use this named anchor in a technique known as the `:target` hack. It's a way to get CSS to respond to a `click` event and avoid using JavaScript to respond to the event. We'll get to the hack in more detail in a bit. First, let's style the window, form, and button.

2. Add the following CSS to style the container, button, form, and the modal window. There's quite a lot going on here so it's broken up with some commentary in between.

```css
/* ---------------------------------- */
/* --- CONTAINER AND BUTTON
/* ---------------------------------- */
.container {
    max-width: 48em;
    margin: 3em auto;
    position: relative;
```

```
    overflow: hidden visible;
}

.btn {
    background: #7a7;
    padding: 1em 2em;
    border: 1px solid #696;
    border-radius: 0.25em;
    text-decoration: none;
    color: #fff;
    float: right;
    position: relative;
    z-index: 5;
}
```

The `.container` is mainly to make the demo more presentable. It's capping the width of everything to 768 pixels (**48em**) and centering itself with **auto** margins. The positioning is so descendant elements can use the `.container div` as a reference point. The **overflow** property and its values come into play later. Just know that you're hiding content that overflows the horizontal boundaries of the `.container`, but you're allowing content that overflows its vertical boundaries.

The styles on the `.btn` class should be self-explanatory. They're mostly for aesthetics. The `.btn` class floats right and has a **relative** positioning with a **z-index** of **5**. The positioning is only so you could add a **z-index**. You'll learn why you set it to a value of **5** momentarily.

```
/* ----------------------------------- */
/* --- FORM
/* ----------------------------------- */
.login input {
    margin-bottom: 1.5em;
    display: block;
}
```

```css
.login input[type=submit] {
    display: block;
    float: left;
    font-size: 0.75em;
    background: #7a7;
    color: #fff;
    padding:1em 2em;
    border: 0;
}

label {
    display: block;
}
```

As with the `.btn` link and the `.container div`, most of the code should be self-explanatory. The form labels and inputs are styled to help lay out the various components of the form and give them some aesthetics.

```css
/* ------------------------------------ */
/* --- MODAL WINDOW
/* ------------------------------------ */
.modal {
    font-size: 1.25em;
    background: #eee;
    color: #000;
    border: 1px solid #ccc;
    border-radius: 3%;
    padding: 7em;
    margin-bottom: 1.5em;
    position: absolute;
    top: 5em;
    right: 0;
```

```
        z-index: 1;

        opacity: 0;

}


.close {

        float: right;

        background: #966;

        border: 1px solid #633;

        margin: 2px 0 0 1em;

        padding: 1em 2em;

        color: #fff;

        text-decoration: none;

        font-size: 0.75em;

}
```

Once again, much of this code is mainly for aesthetics. You float the `.close` link to the right so it's next to the submit button. You position it where the window will display. The main thing to note in this code is the `z-index` of the `.modal` window. It's set to `1`. There's one more `z-index` value to point out and then you'll learn why they're important.

Note that the `opacity` of the `.modal` window is set to `0`. When the page first loads, it is hidden, and this is one easy way to hide the whole window. You also know from the last example that using `opacity` is one way to hide and show elements that all browsers support. It means the modal window will work, even for those browsers that don't support transitions and transforms.

```
/* ------------------------------------- */

/* --- OVERLAY

/* ------------------------------------- */

.overlay {

        position: fixed;

        top: 0;

        left: 0;
```

```
    width: 100%;

    height: 100%;

    background: rgba(128,128,128,0.9);

    opacity: 0;

}
```

The `overlay` is just an empty `div` with a medium background color and slight transparency. Setting the `position`, `top`, and `left` values, along with `100% width` and `height`, ensures the `overlay` reaches all four sides of the screen. Also like the `.modal` window, the `overlay` is hidden by setting its `opacity` to `0`.

You want the `overlay` to open with the `.modal` window. When it does, the `overlay` covers everything on the page, with the exception of the `.modal` window and the form it contains. When it's closed, you want the `overlay` to sit behind the Login button or you won't be able to click the button.

That's why you're using the different `z-index`es. When the page first loads, you want to be able to interact with everything on the page. In this case, that's only the Login button. That's why it gets the highest `z-index`. When the `.modal div` is open, you want it to have the highest `z-index`, and you want the `.overlay div` to have a higher or equal `z-index` to everything else on the page. You'll set this up in the next step.

3. Create the functionality to open and close the `.modal` window and `overlay` with the following code.

But before adding the code, take a moment to think about how you might open the `.modal` window and `overlay`. You need to change the `opacity` of both to `1`, and you need to adjust their `z-index`es. That's simply a few CSS changes. The question is where you add that CSS, and where named anchors and the `:target` hack come in.

Here's the CSS you need.

```
:target .modal {

    opacity: 1;

    z-index: 10;

}
```

```
:target .overlay {

    opacity: 1;

    z-index: 5;

}
```

That doesn't look like much, but it works. The trick is in the `:target` pseudo-element, which matches when the hash in a URL and the `id` of an element are the same. In other words, if the URL of a page is `example.com#hello`, then `:target` will match any element with `id="hello"` as an attribute.

In step 1, you added `#open` to the `href` of the Login `.btn` and also added an `id` of `open` to the `.container div`. This means `:target` will match the `container div` when the URL has `#open` at the end. Clicking the Login `.btn` points to the URL with the hash. The close link inside the `.modal` window sets it back to an empty `#`, which turns off the `:target`.

Notice the new `z-index` values. When the `.modal` and `.overlay divs` are open, the `.modal div` will sit at the top of the stack, with the `.modal div` sitting on top of everything else.

4. Load your code in a browser.

   Congratulations. You now have a working modal window. It's not the most pleasing window, but it works. Some transitional effects would make opening and closing the window a much nicer experience.

5. Add a transition for the change in **opacity** by updating the `.modal` and `.overlay` classes. Changes in the code are highlighted.

```
.modal {

    font-size: 1.25em;

    background: #eee;

    color: #000;

    border: 1px solid #ccc;

    border-radius: 3%;

    padding: 7em;

    margin-bottom: 1.5em;

    position: absolute;
```

NOTE

The `:target` hack is one of several CSS `click` events you can use to respond to visitor actions. There are similar hacks for `:active` and `:focus`. There are also hacks involving checkboxes and radio buttons. If you're interested in learning more about how each works, you can read my article on CSS `click` events at www.vanseodesign.com/css/click-events.

```
      z-index: 1;

      opacity: 0;


      -webkit-transition: opacity 0.5s ease-in-out;

              transition: opacity 0.5s ease-in-out;

   }


   .overlay {

      position: fixed;

      top: 0;

      left: 0;

      width: 100%;

      height: 100%;

      background: rgba(128,128,128,0.9);

      opacity: 0;


      -webkit-transition: opacity 0.5s ease-in-out;

              transition: opacity 0.5s ease-in-out;

   }
```

Hopefully by this point, adding the transitions is old hat. For both the `.modal` and `.overlay` classes, you add a transition for the change in `opacity`. The timing is `ease-in-out` for both.

6. Reload your page. The opening and closing of the window and overlay looks much smoother, but it can be better (**EXAMPLE 6.2**).

Let's slide the `.modal` window in from the right at the same time it's becoming opaque.

7. Adjust your `.modal` and `:target .model` code to include a slide from the right. Additions and changes in the code are highlighted.

```
   .modal {

      font-size: 1.25em;

      background: #eee;
```

```
    color: #000;

    border: 1px solid #ccc;

    border-radius: 3%;

    padding: 7em;

    margin-bottom: 1.5em;

    position: absolute;

    z-index: 1;

    opacity: 0;


    -webkit-transform-origin: center;

        -ms-transform-origin: center;

            transform-origin: center;


    -webkit-transform: translateX(150%);

        -ms-transform: translateX(150%);

            transform: translateX(150%);


    -webkit-transition: opacity 0.25s ease-in-out,
-webkit-transform 0.5s ease-in-out;

            transition: opacity 0.25s ease-in-out,
transform 0.5s ease-in-out;
}

:target .modal {
    opacity: 1;

    z-index: 10;


    -webkit-transform: translateX(0);

        -ms-transform: translateX(0);

            transform: translateX(0);

}
```

Again this is hopefully old hat by now. You use the `translateX()` function of the `transform` property to move the `.modal` window offscreen right and then slide it back in below the Login button when the `:target` URL is the active URL. You adjust the `transform-origin` and then add `transform` to the list of transitions. Once again, browsers that don't support transforms will still be able to use the modal window. They just won't provide quite the same experience.

8. Reload the page again, and observe.

   A Login button appears in the upper right. Clicking it slides the `.modal` window in from the right as it changes from `opacity: 0` to `opacity: 1`. At the same time, the overlay's `opacity` changes from `0` to `1`.

   Hopefully, you agree it's a nicer effect than having both the window and overlay open instantly. It's not the only effect you could use, so let's play a little more and see if we can create some different effects.

NOTE

You're going to create a total of four files and then link them together through a menu so you can compare several effects easily.

9. Make a copy of your file, and name it anything you'd like. Work on the copy for the next step.

10. Change the transitional effect to a card flip (**EXAMPLE 6.3**) by replacing your `.modal` and `:target .modal` code with the following code and adding CSS for the `.modal-container` class. Additions and changes in the code are highlighted.

```
.modal-container {
    -webkit-perspective: 1500px;
       -ms-perspective: 1500px;
           perspective: 1500px;

    position: relative;
    z-index: 10;
}
.modal {
    font-size: 1.25em;
    background: #eee;
    color: #000;
    border: 1px solid #ccc;
```

```
    border-radius: 3%;

    padding: 7em;

    margin-bottom: 1.5em;

    position: absolute;

    z-index: 1;

    opacity: 0;

    -webkit-transform-origin: center;
        -ms-transform-origin: center;
            transform-origin: center;

    -webkit-transform: rotateY(80deg);
        -ms-transform: rotateY(80deg);
            transform: rotateY(80deg);

    -webkit-transition: opacity 0.25s ease-in-out,
    → -webkit-transform 0.25s ease-in-out;

            transition: opacity 0.25s ease-in-out,
            → -webkit-transform 0.25s ease-in-out;
}

:target .modal {
    opacity: 1;
    z-index: 100;

    -webkit-transform: rotateY(0deg);
        -ms-transform: rotateY(0deg);
            transform: rotateY(0deg);
}
```

Once you've worked with transitions and animation more, you'll find it's not that hard to create a new effect. First, you stop the slide by removing the `translateX()` function.

Then to flip the card, you need to add a rotation about the y-axis. After the flip you want the rotation to be 0 degrees so it displays as expected. Prior to the flip, you can experiment. Something a little off perpendicular works well, which is why the code uses **80deg**.

Notice you didn't alter the transition itself, since you were already transitioning over the **transform** property.

This is where the **.modal-container div** comes into play. For the card flip to look more natural, you need to adjust the **perspective**, and that **perspective** needs to be on something that contains what's being flipped. You could add the **perspective** to the **.container div**, but that causes problems in seeing the **.overlay div**. The solution is the **.modal-container div**.

11. Reload the page, and observe the new card flip transition.

    Let's try another effect where the **.modal** window scales up from something very small to its final size (**EXAMPLE 6.4**). Make another copy and work on the new copy for the next step.

12. Replace your CSS for the **.modal** and **:target .modal** selectors with the following CSS. Changes in the code are highlighted.

```
.modal {
    font-size: 1.25em;
    background: #eee;
    color: #000;
    border: 1px solid #ccc;
    border-radius: 3%;
    padding: 7em;
    margin-bottom: 1.5em;

    position: absolute;
    top: 5em;
    right: 0;
    z-index: 1;
```

```
    opacity: 0;

    -webkit-transform-origin: center;
       -ms-transform-origin: center;
           transform-origin: center;

    -webkit-transform: scale(0.1);
       -ms-transform: scale(0.1);
           transform: scale(0.1);

    -webkit-transition: opacity 0.25s ease-in-out,
→ -webkit-transform 0.25s ease-in-out;
           transition: opacity 0.25s ease-in-out,
          → -webkit-transform 0.25s ease-in-out;
}

:target .modal {
    opacity: 1;
    z-index: 10;

    -webkit-transform: scale(1);
       -ms-transform: scale(1);
           transform: scale(1);
}
```

Notice how easy it is to change the effect. You replace the rotation function with a scaling function. Initially, the `.modal` window is one tenth its full size, and it scales up to full size when the window is open.

13. Reload the page, and observe the new effect.

How about reversing the scale? Instead of making it grow to full size, let's make the `.modal` window shrink from very large to normal size (**EXAMPLE 6.5**) and one last time make another copy to work on.

14. Replace your CSS for the `.modal` class with the following CSS. Changes in the code are highlighted.

```css
.modal {
    font-size: 1.25em;
    background: #eee;
    color: #000;
    border: 1px solid #ccc;
    border-radius: 3%;
    padding: 7em;
    margin-bottom: 1.5em;

    position: absolute;
    top: 5em;
    right: 0;
    z-index: 1;

    opacity: 0;

    -webkit-transform-origin: center;
        -ms-transform-origin: center;
            transform-origin: center;

    -webkit-transform: scale(1.5);
        -ms-transform: scale(1.5);
            transform: scale(1.5);

    -webkit-transition: opacity 0.25s ease-in-out,
      -webkit-transform 0.5s ease-in-out;
            transition: opacity 0.25s ease-in-out,
              -webkit-transform 0.5s ease-in-out;
}
```

That was an even easier change. All you had to do was change the initial value in the **scale** function. The example uses 1.5. In practice, you'll use your eye to decide what you like best.

You now have four different modal window documents, each with a different transitional effect. Let's tie them all together with some simple navigation.

15. Replace the HTML from one of your documents with the following HTML. Changes in the code are highlighted.

```html
<div class="container" id="open">
    <div class="modal-container">
        <div class="modal">
            <form class="login">
                <label>Email</label>
                <input type="email" />

                <label>Password</label>
                <input type="password" />

                <input type="submit" value="Login" />
                <a href="#" class="close">Close</a>
            </form>
        </div>
    </div>
    <a href="#open" class="btn">Login</a>

    <ul class="buttons">
        <li><a href="" class="btn-transition
        ⤳ current">Slide In</a></li>
        <li><a href="" class="btn-transition">
        ⤳ Card Flip</a></li>
        <li><a href="" class="btn-transition">
        ⤳ Fade In and Scale Up</a></li>
        <li><a href="" class="btn-transition">
        ⤳ Fade In and Scale Down</a></li>
```

```
    </ul>
    <div class="overlay" id="overlay"></div>
</div>
```

This code adds a list of links with a class of **btn-transition** given to each link. The unordered list gets a class of **buttons**. Notice that the "Slide In" link has an additional class of **current** that you use in the next step to style the **.current** button with a different color.

You need to supply the actual URLs for the **href** attribute with the path to each file.

16. Style the new buttons.

```
.buttons {
    list-style: none;
    margin: 0;
    padding: 0;
    text-align: right;
    float: left;
}

.btn-transition {
    display: block;
    background: #77a;
    padding: 1em 2em;
    border: 1px solid #669;
    border-radius: 0.25em;
    text-decoration: none;
    color: #fff;
    font-size: 1em;
    margin-bottom: 0.5em;
    position: relative;
```

```
    z-index: 1;

}

.current {

    background: #966;

}
```

The majority of this code is for aesthetics: the usual margins, paddings, and background colors. Each button is relatively positioned with a `z-index` of `1`. This keeps them above the `overlay` when the `overlay` is closed and below the `overlay` when it's open.

17. Copy the new HTML and CSS to your other three files.

    You need this code in all your files to connect them. Don't forget to move the `current` class to the correct link for each file.

18. Open any of the files in a browser, and click between them to compare the different effects. Even better, create a few more copies, and see what kind of effects you can create. Then add the new effect to the menu.

You may never choose to use modal windows, and that's OK. But this example showed you how easy it is to add a transitional effect and then modify or add to it to create a different effect.

The majority of the code in this example exists to get everything set up before the transition. The transitions were the easy part. When coding, they'll seem like a small thing you add at the end. However, when you compare the way your elements change with and without them, it is obvious how much the transitional effects improve the experience.

Once again, note that the window is functional even in browsers that don't support transforms or transitions.

Off-canvas Sidebar Navigation

Let's turn back to navigation for the next example. Instead of a drop-down menu, you'll create navigation that slides in from the left side of the screen (**FIGURES 6.5** and **6.6**).

FIGURE 6.5
Off-canvas sidebar navigation closed

FIGURE 6.6
Off-canvas sidebar navigation open

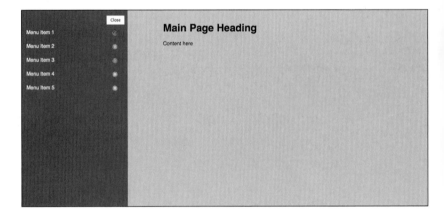

Designing with Progressive Enhancement

Throughout this book I've been saying you should make sure your site functions before you add any transform, transition, or animation. Each should enhance the design, but not be a requirement for making things work. I'm going to break that rule in this example to show you how you can use animation to control opening and closing sidebar navigation.

You should not use the code in this example "as is" in any production work, unless you aren't supporting browsers that lack support for animations and transforms. I'll share thoughts later about how you might re-create this example in a way that you can use in production.

Off-canvas Navigation/Sidebar: Take 1

You've no doubt encountered off-canvas navigation on mobile devices. It's one of the primary ways designers and developers are building navigation for small screens. Moving the navigation off the screen this way is an obvious way to save space (**EXAMPLE 6.6**).

1. Add the following code to a new HTML document:

```
<div class="container">

    <div class="page" id="page">

        <div class="sidebar">

            <button class="toggle" id="toggle">
            → Open</button>

            <ul class="menu">

                <li><a href="" class="one">
                → Menu Item 1</a></li>

                <li><a href="" class="two">
                → Menu Item 2</a></li>

                <li><a href="" class="three">
                → Menu Item 3</a></li>

                <li><a href="" class="four">
                → Menu Item 4</a></li>
```

```
        <li><a href="" class="five">
        → Menu Item 5</a></li>

      </ul>

    </div>

    <div class="main">

      <h1>Page Heading</h1>

      <p>Content here</p>

    </div>

  </div>

</div>
```

This code is the structure for a very simple two-column layout. You can identify the different parts by their class names. The structure contains a sidebar and a main content column. Inside the main content is a heading and a paragraph, but it could be anything you want. The sidebar holds a button and a menu.

Both `.sidebar` and `.main` are wrapped in a `.page div`, which itself is wrapped by a `.container div`. You might think one or the other is unnecessary, but you need both as you'll see.

Two more things to note: First, the `.page div` and the `.toggle` button both have `id`s. You're going to use a little JavaScript to open and close the `.sidebar div`, and these are the elements you need to hook into. Second, each of the links in the `.menu` has a unique class name. These aren't necessary for any functionality in this example—they just give part of each link a different color.

2. Set up the overall layout for the four `div`s.

```
.container {

    width: 100%;

    overflow: hidden;

    background: #ccc;

}
```

```
.page {
    width: 125%;
}

.sidebar {
    width: 27%;
    background: #555;
    padding-top: 1em;
    float: left;
    height: 600px;

}

.main {
    width: 73%;
    float: left;
    height: 600px;
    padding: 1em 25%;
}
```

Note the width of each `div`. The outermost `div` in your HTML is the `.container div`, which is set to **100%** width. **100%** is relative to the HTML body, so `.container` will take up the full width of the screen. Note that `.container` has also been set to hide any overflow.

Just inside the `.container div` is the `.page div`. Its width is set to **125%**, which is relative to the `.container div`. Because overflow on `.container` is `hidden`, 25 percent of the `.page div` is hidden at any given time. By sliding this `div` right and left, you can reveal and hide the sidebar.

The widths of the `.sidebar div` and the `.main div` must add up to 100 percent, which is relative to the `.page div`. The specific values are up to you. This example uses 27 percent and 73 percent respectively, but any values can work as long their sum is 100 percent.

NOTE

In responsive design, you need to adjust these percent values inside your media queries. Setting the `.sidebar div` to **27%** works well on my 1440px monitor. Another value might work better on an 800px wide screen.

The rest of the code floats the `.sidebar div` and the `.main div` to the left and sets some backgrounds and paddings. The height of both `.sidebar` and `.main` are set for this example. In practice, these would be filled with content, but in the example they aren't, so the height is forced by setting it explicitly.

3. Style the `menu` and `.toggle` buttons in the sidebar.

```css
.toggle {
    float: right;
    margin-right: 3%;
    padding: 0.5em 1em;
    background: #fff;
    border: 0;
}

.menu {
    list-style: none;
    padding: 2em 0% 2em 5%;
    margin: 0;
    width: 100%;
    background: #555;
}

.menu a {
    display: block;
    padding: 0.75em 1.5em;
    background: #555;
    text-decoration: none;
    color: #fff;

}
```

```
.menu a:after {

    content: "\25c9";

    float: right;

    margin-right: 3%;

}


.one:after      {color: #f00;}

.two:after      {color: #0f0;}

.three:after    {color: #99f;}

.four:after     {color: #ff0;}

.five:after     {color: #0ff;}


.menu a:hover {

    background: #777;

}
```

Most of this code shouldn't need explanation. In fact, much of it is from the menu styles from the first example in this chapter. The button is floated right. When the menu is in its closed state, a little bit will still show, and floating the button right will ensure it stays visible whether the sidebar is open or closed. The rest of the CSS on the button is just aesthetic styling.

The `.menu` CSS should look familiar; look over it to understand what it's doing. Look specifically at what is going on with the CSS for the `:after` pseudo-element. After every link, `content` is set on this pseudo-element. `\25c9` is unicode representing a fisheye. It looks like a typical list bullet with a circle around it. In a real-world example, you might include icons here instead. Using this technique, the menu will show an icon for each menu item when the sidebar is closed. When the sidebar is open, the text for each of these links appears alongside the icon.

Instead of creating icons, this example places a bullet at the end of each link and gives each a different color to distinguish them. Imagine that each is really an icon representing where the link leads.

4. Add a transform so the page loads with the sidebar offscreen.

5. Load the page now, and you'll notice that the sidebar displays in full.

   You might think the entire .main div is also showing, but an amount equal to the width of the sidebar is actually offscreen right, hidden inside the .container as overflow.

   The current view is an open state, but the page should load in the closed state. Doing that is simple. All you need to do is move the .page div to the left.

   ```
   .page {
       width: 125%;

       -webkit-transform: translateX(-22%);
              transform: translateX(-22%);
   }
   ```

   Adding a translation of -22% along the x-axis to the .page div sets everything in the closed state, which is how the page should load.

6. Reload your page, and observe the new initial state.

   There are two things left to do. You need to add some kind of transition or animation, since that is what this book is about. You also need to add the functionality to the button to open and close the sidebar.

   Let's use animation to do both, and let's start by adding the animation-* properties.

7. Add animation-* properties to the .page div. Changes in the code are highlighted.

   ```
   .page {
       width: 125%;
       -webkit-transform: translateX(-22%);
              transform: translateX(-22%);

       -webkit-animation-name: open;
              animation-name: open;

       -webkit-animation-duration: 0.75s;
              animation-duration: 0.75s;
   ```

```
    -webkit-animation-timing-function: ease-in;
        animation-timing-function: ease-in;

    -webkit-animation-fill-mode: forwards;
        animation-fill-mode: forwards;
```

```
}
```

Although it would be nice to use the shorthand to set the animation, you're going to need to access the value of the **animation-name** property in JavaScript later, and JavaScript needs the individual property. Instead of using shorthand, you can practice using the individual animation properties.

You need to set the **animation-fill-mode** to **forwards**; otherwise after the sidebar completes the open animation, it would instantly go back to its intrinsic state, which in this example is now the closed state.

Let's set up the keyframes.

8. Create the **open** and **close @keyframes** rules.

```
@-webkit-keyframes open {
    0% {
        -webkit-transform: translateX(-22%);
            -ms-transform: translateX(-22%);
                transform: translateX(-22%);
    }

    5% {
        -webkit-transform: translateX(-22%);
            -ms-transform: translateX(-22%);
                transform: translateX(-22%);
    }

    10% {
        -webkit-transform: translateX(-23%);
            -ms-transform: translateX(-23%);
```

```
            transform: translateX(-23%);
    }

    90% {
        -webkit-transform: translateX(-2%);
            -ms-transform: translateX(-2%);
                transform: translateX(-2%);
    }

    95% {
        -webkit-transform: translateX(0%);
            -ms-transform: translateX(0%);
                transform: translateX(0%);
    }

    100% {
        -webkit-transform: translateX(-2%);
            -ms-transform: translateX(-2%);
                transform: translateX(-2%);
    }
}

@keyframes open {
    0% {
        -webkit-transform: translateX(-22%);
            -ms-transform: translateX(-22%);
                transform: translateX(-22%);
    }

    5% {
        -webkit-transform: translateX(-22%);
```

```
        -ms-transform: translateX(-22%);
           transform: translateX(-22%);
  }

  10% {
      -webkit-transform: translateX(-23%);
         -ms-transform: translateX(-23%);
            transform: translateX(-23%);
  }

  90% {
      -webkit-transform: translateX(-2%);
         -ms-transform: translateX(-2%);
            transform: translateX(-2%);
  }

  95% {
      -webkit-transform: translateX(0%);
         -ms-transform: translateX(0%);
            transform: translateX(0%);
  }

  100% {
      -webkit-transform: translateX(-2%);
         -ms-transform: translateX(-2%);
            transform: translateX(-2%);
  }
}
```

The **open @keyframes** rule uses **translateX()** to slide the **.page** to the right. Instead of a single **to** keyframe, anticipation and follow-through is added. The anticipation is **0%** through **10%**, and the follow-through is **90%** to **100%**.

9. Reload your page.

The open animation runs as soon as the page finishes loading, leaving it in the open state. You'll fix this momentarily, but you know if there's an open animation there's going to be a close animation too.

```
@-webkit-keyframes close {
    0% {
        -webkit-transform: translateX(-2%);
            -ms-transform: translateX(-2%);
                transform: translateX(-2%);
    }

    5% {
        -webkit-transform: translateX(0%);
            -ms-transform: translateX(0%);
                transform: translateX(0%);
    }

    10% {
        -webkit-transform: translateX(-2%);
            -ms-transform: translateX(-2%);
                transform: translateX(-2%);
    }

    90% {
        -webkit-transform: translateX(-23%);
            -ms-transform: translateX(-23%);
                transform: translateX(-23%);
    }
```

```
    95% {

        -webkit-transform: translateX(-22%);

            -ms-transform: translateX(-22%);

                transform: translateX(-22%);

    }


    100% {

        -webkit-transform: translateX(-22%);

            -ms-transform: translateX(-22%);

                transform: translateX(-22%);

    }

}


@keyframes close {

    0% {

        -webkit-transform: translateX(-2%);

            -ms-transform: translateX(-2%);

                transform: translateX(-2%);

    }


    5% {

        -webkit-transform: translateX(0%);

            -ms-transform: translateX(0%);

                transform: translateX(0%);

    }


    10% {

        -webkit-transform: translateX(-2%);

            -ms-transform: translateX(-2%);

                transform: translateX(-2%);

    }
```

```
    90% {
        -webkit-transform: translateX(-23%);
            -ms-transform: translateX(-23%);
                transform: translateX(-23%);
    }

    95% {
        -webkit-transform: translateX(-22%);
            -ms-transform: translateX(-22%);
                transform: translateX(-22%);
    }

    100% {
        -webkit-transform: translateX(-22%);
            -ms-transform: translateX(-22%);
                transform: translateX(-22%);
    }
}
```

The `close @keyframes` rule is simply a reverse of the `open @keyframes` rule. It has keyframes at the same percentages, but the values are in reverse.

To add the ability for the button to open and close the sidebar, you're going to use JavaScript to change the `animation-name` property. Don't worry. It's JavaScript that is similar to what you've seen already in this book. Ready?

10. Add the JavaScript to make this all work:

```
<script>
var init = function() {

    var page = document.getElementById('page');
    var toggle = document.getElementById('toggle');

    toggle.addEventListener( 'click', function(){
```

```
    var webkitAnimationName =
    → window.getComputedStyle(page).getPropertyValue
    → ("-webkit-animation-name");

    var animationName = window.getComputedStyle(page).
    → getPropertyValue("animation-name");


    if(webkitAnimationName != ""){

        ((webkitAnimationName != "open") ?
        → (page.style.webkitAnimationName = "open",
        → toggle.firstChild.data = "Close" ) :
        → (page.style.webkitAnimationName =
        →"close", toggle.firstChild.data = "Open" ));

    }


    if(animationName != null){

        ((animationName != "open")   ?
        → (page.style.animationName = "open",
        → toggle.firstChild.data = "Close" ) :
        → (page.style.animationName = "close",
        → toggle.firstChild.data = "Open" ));

    }

}, false);


};


window.addEventListener('DOMContentLoaded', init, false);
</script>
```

The last line adds an event listener for when the page finishes loading and calls the **init** function when it does.

The function grabs the elements with **ids** of **page** and **toggle** (which represent the **.page div** and the **.toggle** button). The function includes another event listener for when the **toggle** button is clicked, which sends you to the inner function.

Inside the function, you set two more variables:

```
var webkitAnimationName = window.getComputedStyle(page).
→ getPropertyValue("-webkit-animation-name");

var animationName = window.getComputedStyle(page).
→ getPropertyValue("animation-name");
```

Each grabs the current value of the `animation-name` (or `-webkit-animation-name`) property. These two variables are for convenience, since they're easier to type again than `window.getComputedStyle(page).getPropertyValue("animation-name");` and its `-webkit` variation.

NOTE

Unfortunately,
`window.getComputedStyle`
doesn't work in IE8.
Fortunately, there's a
fix you can find at http://
snipplr.com/view/13523.

The next two lines of code need more explanation. Let's walk through the non-Webkit block of code. Inside each block is the ternary operator, which is in the form

```
(condition) ? run this code if yes : run this code if no;
```

The condition is

```
(animationName != open)
```

It checks the current value of `animationName` and tests if it's equal to something other than `open`.

If the answer is yes, the following code runs:

```
(page.style.animationName = "open",
→ toggle.firstChild.data = "Close" )
```

It sets the `animation-name` value to `open` and then changes the button text to "Close."

However, if the answer to the condition is no, the following code runs, which sets the `animation-name` value to `close` and the button text to "Open."

```
(page.style.animationName = "close",
→ toggle.firstChild.data = "Open" )
```

In other words, whenever the sidebar is closed, the button should read Open. Clicking it runs the open animation, which leaves the sidebar in its open state. It also changes the button text to Close. When the sidebar is in the open state, clicking the Close button runs the close animation and changes the button text back to Open.

Each block of code wraps the ternary operator inside an `if` statement. This is to fix an issue with Webkit browsers. You might expect Webkit browsers to ignore the non-Webkit block of code, but they don't. They set the variable `animationName` to `null`, and since `null` does not equal `open`, the non-Webkit ternary operator runs. It doesn't affect the page moving left and right, but it does cause problems in changing the button text from Open to Close.

The solution is to wrap the ternary line of code in the `if` statement.

```
animationName != null {

    ternary operator

}
```

Since only Webkit browsers are setting `animationName` to `null`, you test to make sure `animationName` has any other value before letting the ternary operator run. That prevents Webkit browsers from running the code it shouldn't run, which fixes the button text issue.

The code wraps a similar `if` statement around the Webkit line of code, although it wasn't necessary. The non-Webkit browsers set `webkitAnimationName` to an empty string instead of `null`, so the condition is a little different, but the code is doing the same thing.

11. Reload the page, and test that everything is working.

Click the button to move the `.page div` left and right, effectively opening and closing the sidebar.

There's still one problem, and that's how the open animation runs once the page loads. To correct this, all you need to do is change the value you initially give to the `animation-name` property to something other than `open`. My first thought was to set it to `close`.

```
-webkit-animation-name: close;
        animation-name: close;
```

It's an option, but it runs the close animation when the page first loads. This isn't an awful experience. It lets the viewer know that there is a menu off to the side. Watching it close should cue the viewer that it can also be opened. However, because this animation runs every time the visitor clicks to a new page of the site, it would probably get very tiresome very fast.

Instead, let's set the `animation-name` value to something that doesn't have an `@keyframes` rule associated with it. You'll use the word "hello," which is a completely arbitrary choice.

12. Replace your CSS for the `.page div` with the following CSS. Changes in the code are highlighted.

```
.page {
    width: 125%;
    -webkit-transform: translateX(-22%);
            transform: translateX(-22%);

    -webkit-animation-name: hello;
            animation-name: hello;

    -webkit-animation-duration: 0.75s;
            animation-duration: 0.75s;

    -webkit-animation-timing-function: ease-in;
            animation-timing-function: ease-in;

    -webkit-animation-fill-mode: forwards;
            animation-fill-mode: forwards;

}
```

Since there is no `@keyframes hello` rule, no animation runs automatically. Your JavaScript checks for the not open (`!= "open"`) condition, which includes both `close` and now `hello`.

13. Reload your page one last time, and check to make sure it works.

The page loads with your sidebar in the closed state. Clicking the button opens and closes the sidebar and changes the button text to reflect what action it'll perform next.

Reworking the Example for Progressive Enhancement

Let me address how you might instead re-create this example in a way that works in browsers that don't support animations or transforms. First if you use this method, the sidebar navigation should always remain open. Technically it works, but it's unlikely to work quite how you want. You could make some adjustments to the layout so it would work, and if the menu is always open, you'd probably want to remove the Open/Close button.

However, you could also leave the layout as is and change from using an animation to control the opening and closing and instead use transitions the way you have been so far in this chapter. Instead of the animation, you might use margins (negative to slide offscreen) or maybe use positioning and adjust the left or right values. Anything that can move the `.page div` left and right will work.

Then in your JavaScript, you'd read the value of the property you're using to move the `.page div` and change it the same way you did in this example. Finally, you'd add a transition to smooth the change.

Off-canvas Navigation/Sidebar: Take 2

Let's try a variation of the previous example. Instead of sliding the entire `.page div` with both `.sidebar` and `.main divs` moving with it, let's leave the main content area alone and just slide the sidebar off and on the canvas (**EXAMPLE 6.7**).

Much of this example repeats what was in the previous example. Copy the previous example to a new HTML file. It'll be easier to modify the previous code than start from scratch.

1. Replace the HTML from the previous example with the following HTML:

```
<div class="container">
    <div class="sidebar" id="sidebar">
        <button class="toggle" id="toggle">Open</button>
        <ul class="menu">
            <li><a href="" class="one">
            → Menu Item 1</a></li>
            <li><a href="" class="two">
            → Menu Item 2</a></li>
```

NOTE

Again the same caveat applies. Don't use the code in this example as is in your production work. It uses animation to open and close the sidebar navigation, which won't work in all browsers. You can use the method described in "Off-canvas Navigation/ Sidebar: Take 1" to make it work and still have a smooth transition.

```
            <li><a href="" class="three">
            → Menu Item 3</a></li>

            <li><a href="" class="four">
            → Menu Item 4</a></li>

            <li><a href="" class="five">
            → Menu Item 5</a></li>

        </ul>

    </div>

    <div class="main">

        <h1>Heading</h1>

        <p>Some page content</p>

    </div>

</div>
```

Alternatively, you can remove the `.page div` from the previous example because that's all that changed. Since you are sliding only the `.sidebar`, the wrapping `.page` is no longer necessary.

2. Modify the `.sidebar` and `.main` divs. Changes in the code are highlighted.

```
.sidebar {

    width: 27%;

    background: #555;

    padding-top: 1em;

    position: absolute;

    height: 600px;

}


.main {

    width: 100%;

    float: left;

    height: 600px;

    padding: 1em 25% 1em 35%;

}
```

The changes are minimal. You want the `.sidebar` to move independently in this example. The easiest way to do that is to add some absolute positioning that takes the sidebar out of the normal document flow.

Removing `.sidebar` from the normal document flow means the `.main div` slides all the way to the left to fill the space it identifies as vacated. To compensate, you change the `.main width` to `100%` and adjust the left and right `padding` to place the content roughly where it was before.

Would you believe you're almost finished?

3. Move the `transform` and `animation` that were previously on the `.page div` to the `.sidebar div`. Modify the value in the `translateX()` function. And feel free to remove the `.page` code.

```
.sidebar {
    width: 27%;
    background: #555;
    padding-top: 1em;
    position: absolute;
    height: 600px;

    -webkit-transform: translateX(-80%);
            transform: translateX(-80%);

    -webkit-animation-name: hello;
            animation-name: hello;

    -webkit-animation-duration: 0.75s;
            animation-duration: 0.75s;

    -webkit-animation-timing-function: ease-in;
            animation-timing-function: ease-in;

    -webkit-animation-fill-mode: forwards;
            animation-fill-mode: both;
```

```
        -webkit-animation-play-state: running;
            animation-play-state: running;
}
```

There's no `.page div` here, but the animation and initial transform you used is almost what you want on the `.sidebar div`. The one change is the value of the `translateX()` function. In the previous example, you were setting a percentage of the `.page div`, and now you're setting a percentage of the `.sidebar div`, so the value needs to be larger.

4. Modify the values in the `@keyframes` rules. Changes in the code are highlighted.

```
@-webkit-keyframes open {
    0% {
        -webkit-transform: translateX(-80%);
            -ms-transform: translateX(-80%);
                transform: translateX(-80%);
    }

    5% {
        -webkit-transform: translateX(-80%);
            -ms-transform: translateX(-80%);
                transform: translateX(-80%);
    }

    10% {
        -webkit-transform: translateX(-82%);
            -ms-transform: translateX(-82%);
                transform: translateX(-82%);
    }
```

```
90% {

    -webkit-transform: translateX(-2%);

        -ms-transform: translateX(-2%);

            transform: translateX(-2%);

}

95% {

    -webkit-transform: translateX(0%);

        -ms-transform: translateX(0%);

            transform: translateX(0%);

}

100% {

    -webkit-transform: translateX(-2%);

        -ms-transform: translateX(-2%);

            transform: translateX(-2%);

}

}

@keyframes open {

    0% {

        -webkit-transform: translateX(-80%);

            -ms-transform: translateX(-80%);

                transform: translateX(-80%);

    }

    5% {

        -webkit-transform: translateX(-80%);

            -ms-transform: translateX(-80%);

                transform: translateX(-80%);

    }
```

```
    10% {
        -webkit-transform: translateX(-82%);
           -ms-transform: translateX(-82%);
               transform: translateX(-82%);
    }

    90% {
        -webkit-transform: translateX(-2%);
           -ms-transform: translateX(-2%);
               transform: translateX(-2%);
    }

    95% {
        -webkit-transform: translateX(0%);
           -ms-transform: translateX(0%);
               transform: translateX(0%);
    }

    100% {
        -webkit-transform: translateX(-2%);
           -ms-transform: translateX(-2%);
               transform: translateX(-2%);
    }
}

@-webkit-keyframes close {
    0% {
        -webkit-transform: translateX(-2%);
           -ms-transform: translateX(-2%);
               transform: translateX(-2%);
    }
```

```
    5% {
        -webkit-transform: translateX(0%);
          -ms-transform: translateX(0%);
              transform: translateX(0%);
    }

    10% {
        -webkit-transform: translateX(-2%);
          -ms-transform: translateX(-2%);
              transform: translateX(-2%);
    }

    90% {
        -webkit-transform: translateX(-83%);
          -ms-transform: translateX(-83%);
              transform: translateX(-83%);
    }

    95% {
        -webkit-transform: translateX(-82%);
          -ms-transform: translateX(-82%);
              transform: translateX(-82%);
    }

    100% {
        -webkit-transform: translateX(-80%);
          -ms-transform: translateX(-80%);
              transform: translateX(-80%);
    }
}
```

```css
@keyframes close {
    0% {
        -webkit-transform: translateX(-2%);
            -ms-transform: translateX(-2%);
                transform: translateX(-2%);
    }

    5% {
        -webkit-transform: translateX(0%);
            -ms-transform: translateX(0%);
                transform: translateX(0%);
    }

    10% {
        -webkit-transform: translateX(-2%);
            -ms-transform: translateX(-2%);
                transform: translateX(-2%);
    }

    90% {
        -webkit-transform: translateX(-83%);
            -ms-transform: translateX(-83%);
                transform: translateX(-83%);
    }

    95% {
        -webkit-transform: translateX(-82%);
            -ms-transform: translateX(-82%);
                transform: translateX(-82%);
    }
```

```
100% {
    -webkit-transform: translateX(-80%);
        -ms-transform: translateX(-80%);
            transform: translateX(-80%);
    }
}
```

About half the values change from the previous example to this one. Other-wise the keyframes are doing the same thing.

5. Replace your JavaScript code with the following. Changes in the code are highlighted.

```
<script>
var init = function() {

    var sidebar = document.getElementById('sidebar');
    var toggle = document.getElementById('toggle');

    toggle.addEventListener( 'click', function(){

        var webkitAnimationName =
        → window.getComputedStyle(sidebar).
        → getPropertyValue("-webkit-animation-name");
        var animationName =
        → window.getComputedStyle(sidebar).
        → getPropertyValue("animation-name");

        if(webkitAnimationName != ""){
            ((webkitAnimationName != "open") ?
            → (sidebar.style.webkitAnimationName =
            →"open", toggle.firstChild.data = "Close" )
            →: (sidebar.style.webkitAnimationName =
            →"close", toggle.firstChild.data =
            →"Open" ));

        }
```

```
if(animationName != null){

    ((animationName != "open") ?
    (sidebar.style.animationName = "open",
    → toggle.firstChild.data = "Close" ) :
    → (sidebar.style.animationName = "close",
    → toggle.firstChild.data = "Open" ));

}


false);

};


window.addEventListener('DOMContentLoaded', init, false);
</script>
```

It's the same JavaScript from the previous example, with the exception that all mentions of **page** have been changed to **sidebar**.

6. Load the new file in a browser, and check that it's working.

This example should look similar to the previous one. The difference is that the **.main div** never moves. Only the **.sidebar div** moves left and right, appearing to open and close. Between the two methods, this is the one I prefer. It feels more natural.

One thing you might do to extend this example is to make it clearer that the **.sidebar div** is sliding in on top of the **.main div**. A couple of years ago the obvious choice would have been adding a drop shadow to the **.sidebar**. Today's flatter trend would sooner reach for transparency and set the **.sidebar** to something less than **opacity: 1.** Another option might be to have some text or other visual element be partially covered when the **.sidebar** opens.

One more example to go. Let's create a content switcher.

Content Switcher

There's one last example to work through: a content switcher (**FIGURE 6.7**), which is similar to an image slider. It's called content because you can fill it with more than images, and switcher because it doesn't automatically slide images into view. The name avoids calling it an image slider because studies tend to show most people never look beyond the first image in the slider. However, the example does use class names and an `id` of `slider`, because it accurately describes the action that's taking place (**EXAMPLE 6.8**).

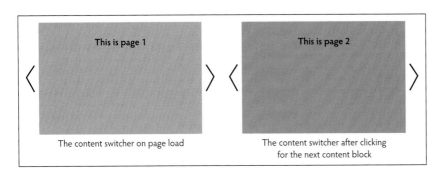

The content switcher on page load

The content switcher after clicking
for the next content block

FIGURE 6.7
Content switcher

Through this example, you'll see how quick and easy it can be to create different transitional effects.

1. Create a new document with the following HTML:

```
<div class="container">
    <div class="slider" id="slider">
        <div class="content one" id="one">
            <h1>This is page 1</h1>
        </div>
        <div class="content two" id="two">
            <h1>This is page 2</h1>
        </div>
        <div class="content three" id="three">
            <h1>This is page 3</h1>
        </div>
```

```
<div class="content four" id="four">
    <h1>This is page 4</h1>
</div>
</div>
<div class="nav">
    <a class="prev" id="prev" href="#">&#12296;</a>
    <a class="next" id="next" href="#">&#12297;</a>
</div>
</div>
```

In this code, you have four **divs**, each with a class of **content**. Each **div** gets a unique class (**one**, **two**, **three**, or **four**) as well as a corresponding **id**. Each contains a heading with text identifying the **div** as one of four pages. All four **divs** are wrapped by a **.slider div**.

In addition to the **.slider** and its **divs** are navigation links for previous and next, each with a class and **id** that describes which is which. The anchor text of the links are HTML entities for left and right angle brackets that are taller and narrower than the one on your keyboard.

Everything is wrapped by a **.container div**.

2. Style the components of the **content** window.

```
.container {
    max-width: 600px;
    margin: 2em auto;
    overflow: hidden;
}

.slider {
    width: 2400px;
    margin-left: 0px;
}
```

```
.content {

    width: 600px;

    height: 400px;

    float: left;

    text-align: center;

    padding: 2em 0;

    border-radius: 1%;

}


.one   { background: #c66; } /* -- red -- */

.two   { background: #6c6; } /* -- green -- */

.three { background: #66c; } /* -- blue -- */

.four  { background: #cc6; } /* -- yellow -- */
```

Think a moment about what's going on in this code. The majority of it reveals how you're going to set up the change from one `div` of content to the next.

You set the `.content div` to have dimensions of 600 pixels by 400 pixels. Each content block is floated `left`. The remaining CSS for the class makes what's inside a little more presentable. Each of the four `div`s is also given a different background color so you can tell them apart.

Your four `.content div`s are contained by a `.slider div` that's 2400 pixels wide. That works out nice since 4×600 pixels = 2400 pixels. The slider also gets a `margin-left` of `0px`, which isn't doing anything at the moment, but it should clue you in to how you'll be switching content blocks.

Finally, the outermost `.container div` is given a `width` of `600px` (the same as your content) with its `overflow` set to `hidden`. In other words, your `.slider div` will reveal `600px` of itself (the exact width of your content) at any one time, with the rest being hidden. Setting the `left` and `right` margin to `auto` (`margin: 2em auto;`) centers the `.container` horizontally on the screen and pushes it down a bit from the top.

3. Style the navigation with the following code:

```
.nav {
    font-size: 5em;
    width: 800px;
    position: absolute;
    margin: 1.5em 0 0 -100px;
}

.nav a {
    text-decoration: none;
    color: #444;
    font-weight: bold;
}

.prev {float: left;}
.next {float: right;}
```

Both links are contained in a `nav` element and floated inside the `.nav div` to the `left` and `right` with the `.nav div` itself wider than the `.container div`. This allows the angle brackets to display to the sides of the `.container`. The absolute positioning takes the `.nav div` outside the normal document flow. Otherwise, it would display below the `.content div`.

The next step is making this work. In step 2, you used the `margin-left` property to control which `div` of content displays in the visible `.container` window. Intrinsically, the `.slider div` has `margin-left: 0` set. That shows the first content block. Adjusting the value shows the other `.content divs` in the `.container` window:

* To show content block **one**, use `margin-left: 0;`.

* To show content block **two**, use `margin-left: -600px;`.

* To show content block **three**, use `margin-left: -12000px;`.

* To show content block **four**, use `margin-left: -1800px;`.

But how do you do that? You need to first grab the current value of the `margin-left` property. If someone clicks next when the value is set to `-1200px`, then block `three` is showing, and you need to change the value to `-1800px` to hide block `three` and show block `four`.

To do this, you're going to use JavaScript. First, you read the current value, and then you change the value. This code uses some new JavaScript code, but it will be explained.

4. Add the following JavaScript between `<script></script>` tags in the `head` of your document.

```
<script>
var init = function() {

    var slider = document.getElementById('slider');

    var one = document.getElementById('one');

    var two = document.getElementById('two');

    var three = document.getElementById('three');

    var four = document.getElementById('four');


    var next = document.getElementById("next");

    var prev = document.getElementById("prev");

}


window.addEventListener('DOMContentLoaded', init, false);

</script>
```

This code should be familiar. It sets up an event listener that listens for the page to complete loading. You need to read and change the `margin-left` value in the `.slider div`, so you grab a hook to the element. You want to be able to hook into each of the content blocks so you need to set variables for each. You want to know when the next and previous links have been clicked, so grab hooks to them as well.

5. Add the following to the end of your `init` function:

```
next.addEventListener( 'click', function(){

    var margin = window.getComputedStyle(slider).
    → getPropertyValue("margin-left");

}, false);
```

This code listens for a click on the next link (you'll create a similar func-tion for the previous link) and creates a function when it's clicked. You've seen this in all the JavaScript examples to this point.

The `window.getComputedStyle(slider).getPropertyValue("margin-left")` is what actually gets the value of the `margin-left` property. You saw similar code in the off-canvas examples. It gets the computed style and not the one intrinsically set. It's the actual current value.

Now that you know the current value, you can change it to show the next or previous `.content div`.

6. Add the following logic to the end of your `init` function to change the `margin-left` property value based on its current value. Add the new highlighted code.

```
var margin = window.getComputedStyle(slider).
→ getPropertyValue("margin-left");

    switch (margin) {
        case "0px":
            slider.style.marginLeft = "-600px";
            break;
        case "-600px":
            slider.style.marginLeft = "-1200px";
            break;
```

```
        case "-1200px":
            slider.style.marginLeft = "-1800px";
            break;
        case "-1800px":
            slider.style.marginLeft = "0px";
            break;
    }
```

You could run a series of **if else** statements, but a **switch** statement is easier when you have multiple **if else** statements. If this is new to you, what's going on is that the code first checks the value of the **margin** variable. If the value is **0px**, it runs the code in **case "0px":**. If the value is **-1200px**, it runs the code in **case "-1200px":**. Once the code reaches a **break;** statement, it breaks out of the **switch** statement so the code in the next case doesn't run.

Changing the value of the **margin-left** property is a little easier than reading it:

```
slider.style.marginLeft = "-600px";
```

Everything is now working whenever the visitor clicks to see the next content block. You still need to set up the previous link. Fortunately it's similar to the code you just added for the next link. The only differences are some of the values.

7. Add the following code below the code in step 6:

```
prev.addEventListener( 'click', function(){

    var margin = window.getComputedStyle(slider).
    → getPropertyValue("margin-left");

    switch (margin) {
        case "0px":
            slider.style.marginLeft = "-1800px";
            break;
```

```
        case "-600px":
            slider.style.marginLeft = "0px";
            break;
        case "-1200px":
            slider.style.marginLeft = "-600px";
            break;
        case "-1800px":
            slider.style.marginLeft = "-1200px";
            break;
    }
```

The only thing left to add is the transition.

8. Replace the CSS code for the `.slider` class with the following code. Changes in the code are highlighted.

```
.slider {
    width: 2400px;
    margin-left: 0px;

    -webkit-transition: margin-left 0.5s ease-in-out;
          transition: margin-left 0.5s ease-in-out;
}
```

You add a transition over the `margin-left` property, and set its duration to `0.5s` and its timing function to `ease-in-out`.

9. Load your document in a browser.

Clicking either link moves the `.slider div` to reveal a different content block. Instead of an instant change, the `.slider` transitions to the right or left. It works, but you can do more. Let's add a couple more changes to transition over.

Let's use opacity and scaling. The `.content div` that's showing should have an `opacity` of `1` and a `transform` value of `scale(1);`. Those not showing should be set to `opacity: 0` and `transform: scale(0);`. When all the changes transition, it'll create a more interesting effect than just sliding left or right.

10. Replace your CSS code for classes `.one`, `.two`, `.three`, and `.four` with the following CSS code:

```
.one {
    background: #c66;
    opacity: 1;

    -webkit-transform: scale(1);
        -ms-transform: scale(1);
            transform: scale(1);

    -webkit-transition: opacity 0.5s ease-in-out,
    → -webkit-transform 0.5s ease-in-out;
            transition: opacity 0.5s ease-in-out,
            →  transform 0.5s ease-in-out;
}

.two {
    background: #6c6;
    opacity: 0;

    -webkit-transform: scale(0);
        -ms-transform: scale(0);
            transform: scale(0);

    -webkit-transition: opacity 0.5s ease-in-out,
    → -webkit-transform 0.5s ease-in-out;
```

```
            transition: opacity 0.5s ease-in-out,
          → transform 0.5s ease-in-out;
    }

    .three {
        background: #66c;
        opacity: 0;

        -webkit-transform: scale(0);
           -ms-transform: scale(0);
               transform: scale(0);

        -webkit-transition: opacity 0.5s ease-in-out,
        →-webkit-transform 0.5s ease-in-out;
                transition: opacity 0.5s ease-in-out,
              → transform 0.5s ease-in-out;
    }

    .four {
        background: #cc6;
        opacity: 0;

        -webkit-transform: scale(0);
           -ms-transform: scale(0);
               transform: scale(0);

        -webkit-transition: opacity 0.5s ease-in-out,
        →-webkit-transform 0.5s ease-in-out;
                transition: opacity 0.5s ease-in-out,
              → transform 0.5s ease-in-out;
    }
```

For each of the four `.content` divs, you add an **opacity** and a **scale** function. The `.one div` gets an **opacity** of **1** and is scaled to full size. The other **divs** have **0 opacity** and **scale** to **0**. You also add opacity to the transition list in addition to the one already there for the transform.

Next you have to update your JavaScript to change the opacity and scaling values when changing the value of the **translateX()** function on the `.slider div`.

11. Modify the function that runs when the next link is clicked. Changes in the code are highlighted.

```
next.addEventListener( 'click', function(){

        var margin = window.getComputedStyle(slider).
     → getPropertyValue("margin-left");

    switch (margin) {
      case "0px":
            slider.style.marginLeft = "-600px";
            one.style.opacity = "0";
            one.style.webkitTransform = "scale(0)";
            one.style.transform = "scale(0)";
            two.style.opacity = "1";
            two.style.webkitTransform = "scale(1)";
            two.style.transform = "scale(1)";
            break;
      case "-600px":
            slider.style.marginLeft = "-1200px";
            two.style.opacity = "0";
            two.style.webkitTransform = "scale(0)";
            two.style.transform = "scale(0)";
            three.style.opacity = "1";
```

```
                three.style.webkitTransform = "scale(1)";
                three.style.transform = "scale(1)";
                break;
            case "-1200px":
                slider.style.marginLeft = "-1800px";
                three.style.opacity = "0";
                three.style.webkitTransform = "scale(0)";
                three.style.transform = "scale(0)";
                four.style.opacity = "1";
                four.style.webkitTransform = "scale(1)";
                four.style.transform = "scale(1)";
                break;
            case "-1800px":
                slider.style.marginLeft = "0px";
                four.style.opacity = "0";
                four.style.webkitTransform = "scale(0)";
                four.style.transform = "scale(0)";
                one.style.opacity = "1";
                one.style.webkitTransform = "scale(1)";
                one.style.transform = "scale(1)";
                break;
        }
    }, false);
```

It looks like a lot, but if you've understood what's been going on to this point, seeing what's going on in the code here should be easy. As each content block slides outside the window, its **opacity** changes to **0** and it scales to **0**. Each content block entering the window has its **opacity** set to **1** and its scale to full size.

The function that runs when the previous link is clicked is similarly modified:

```
prev.addEventListener( 'click', function(){

    var margin = window.getComputedStyle(slider).
  → getPropertyValue("margin-left");

    switch (margin) {
        case "0px":
            slider.style.marginLeft = "-1800px";
            one.style.opacity = "0";
            one.style.webkitTransform = "scale(0)";
            one.style.transform = "scale(0)";
            four.style.opacity = "1";
            four.style.webkitTransform = "scale(1)";
            four.style.transform = "scale(1)";
            break;
        case "-600px":
            slider.style.marginLeft = "0px";
            two.style.opacity = "0";
            two.style.webkitTransform = "scale(0)";
            two.style.transform = "scale(0)";
            one.style.opacity = "1";
            one.style.webkitTransform = "scale(1)";
            one.style.transform = "scale(1)";
            break;
        case "-1200px":
            slider.style.marginLeft = "-600px";
            three.style.opacity = "0";
            three.style.webkitTransform = "scale(0)";
```

```
            three.style.transform = "scale(0)";

            two.style.opacity = "1";

            two.style.webkitTransform = "scale(1)";

            two.style.transform = "scale(1)";

            break;

      case "-1800px":

            slider.style.marginLeft = "-1200px";

            four.style.opacity = "0";

            four.style.webkitTransform = "scale(0)";

            four.style.transform = "scale(0)";

            three.style.opacity = "1";

            three.style.webkitTransform = "scale(1)";

            three.style.transform = "scale(1)";

            break;

      }

}, false);
```

12. Reload the page with the new code, and observe the difference. It's a much more interesting effect with both **opacity** and the **scale** function added.

This has been a long example, but let's do one last thing. Often when an image or block of content is presented as is done here, you can hover over it and have some additional information appear. That's what you'll do now.

13. Replace your HTML with the following HTML. Changes in the code are highlighted.

```
<div class="container">

    <div class="slider" id="slider">

        <div class="content one" id="one">

            <h1>This is page 1</h1>

            <p class="additional">This is some
            → additional information about page 1 that
            → can be revealed on hover.</p>
```

```
    </div>

    <div class="content two" id="two">

        <h1>This is page 2</h1>

        <p class="additional">This is some
        → additional information about page 2 that
        → can be revealed on hover.</p>

    </div>

    <div class="content three" id="three">

        <h1>This is page 3</h1>

        <p class="additional">This is some
        → additional information about page 3 that
        → can be revealed on hover.</p>

    </div>

    <div class="content four" id="four">

        <h1>This is page 4</h1>

        <p class="additional">This is some
        → additional information about page 4 that
        → can be revealed on hover.</p>

    </div>

  </div>

  <nav>

      <a class="prev" id="prev" href="#">&#12296;</a>

      <a class="next" id="next" href="#">&#12297;</a>

  </nav>

</div>
```

All you're doing here is adding a paragraph below each heading. Each paragraph is given a class of `additional`. Feel free to be more creative with what you use for text.

14. Add the following CSS to your file:

```
.additional {
    padding: 1em 25%;
    position: absolute;
    bottom: -6em;
    background: rgba(0,0,0,0.3);
    color: #eee;
    font-weight: 100;

    -webkit-transition: bottom 0.5s ease-in;
            transition: bottom 0.5s ease-in;
}


.content:hover .additional {
    bottom: -1em;
}
```

First you set the `.additional` paragraph to have **absolute** positioning. Since this change on hover is the only way to reveal the additional information, you should use something that you know works in all browsers. This code uses the `bottom` property. A value of `-6em` hides the `.additional` paragraph.

Here, you use the **rgba** value to add a background color. The value inside shows black with 30 percent opacity. That creates a background that allows what's below to shine through. It appears to darken whatever color is already present.

Finally, you add a transition for the change in the `bottom` property.

15. Reload your page, and hover over the `.content` blocks. The `.additional` paragraph slides up from the bottom.

There's still one little bit not working. If you hover over any of the `.content divs` in between the next and previous links, nothing happens. To fix this, you have to revisit some code from earlier in this example.

16. Add positioning and a `z-index` to the `.slider div`. Changes in the code are highlighted.

```
.slider {
    width: 2400px;
    position: relative;
    z-index: 1;
    margin-left: 0;

    -webkit-transition: -webkit-transform 0.5s
    ⇥ ease-in-out;
            transition: transform 0.5s ease-in-out;
}
```

Remember way back when you started this example, you set the **nav** element to **position: absolute**. That automatically gave it a **z-index** of 0, which actually places it on top of everything else. When you thought you were hovering over the `.content div`, you were really hovering over the **nav** element.

To correct the problem, you need to move the `.slider` above the **nav** element. Give it some relative positioning, and set its **z-index** to something greater than 0 (1 will do), and with that change you're finished.

17. Reload the page in your browser one last time (I promise it's really the last time), and observe the final version of the example.

Hopefully, you agree the effect is nicer than before when you weren't adding any transitions. With or without the transforms and transitions you used, the content switcher still works.

What I also hope you take away from this example is the ability to combine transitions on different properties into a single effect. Don't limit yourself to changing one thing. Sometimes a single property change is effective, but sometimes a combination of property changes is more effective. Once you have a working page, adding effects through transitions and animations is easy, so experiment and explore.

Summary

I hope the examples have given you some ideas for how to work with transforms, transitions, and animations in real-world practice. In the "Resources" appendix, you'll find links to sites with more examples that can stoke your imagination.

What's most important to take away from the examples in this chapter is that each is built to function in browsers that don't support transforms, transitions, and animations, and each design is extended to include the enhancements for browsers that do support them. This ensures your designs work in as many browsers as possible, while providing an enhanced experience for the more capable browsers.

CHAPTER 7

CLOSING THOUGHTS

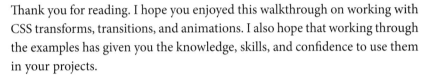

Thank you for reading. I hope you enjoyed this walkthrough on working with CSS transforms, transitions, and animations. I also hope that working through the examples has given you the knowledge, skills, and confidence to use them in your projects.

Remember although browser support is very good, it's not perfect. You'll have to decide which browsers you need to support and use polyfills where available and necessary for a particular browser. Still, there's little reason to hesitate.

The techniques in this book are best applied as simple changes over time. Make a button glow when hovered or clicked. Have information slide on and off the page. Add small touches of delight to your site with subtle and useful motion. These touches add up to more than the sum of their parts. Use the ideas in this book to combine techniques and create your own effects.

Progressive Enhancement

At the start of this book I mentioned that there are several layers to designing a positive experience:

* Functional—The design works and meets basic functional needs.

* Reliable—The design has stable and consistent performance.

* Usable—The design is easy to use.

* Proficiency—The design empowers people to do more and do it better.

* Creativity—The design is aesthetically beautiful with innovative interactions.

The techniques in this book can be applied to the last three layers. They can make your site more usable by highlighting important information and directing viewers to it. They can provide cues to additional information, making users more proficient. And their creative possibilities are limited only by your imagination. But remember: What you add to the last three layers shouldn't break either of the first two.

You want to build websites that work in as many browsers and devices as possible. At a minimum, the site needs to work. On top of this working site, you add layers for those devices and browsers that are more capable. For browsers that support transforms, transitions, and animations, add each in a way that the site isn't dependent on them working. Make sure people using non-supporting browsers can still access all your information and do everything people using a supporting browser can. The experience may be different, but everything should work for everyone.

NOTE

I used a small amount of JavaScript throughout this book as well. It isn't necessary for working with animation, but it can add a measure of control and granularity. Most of the time you used JavaScript to hook into HTML elements and changed the value on one or more CSS properties. You'll find it useful to use JavaScript to add, remove, and modify the classes on an element.

With the exception of the off-canvas sidebar/menu in Chapter 6, I presented the examples with the idea of progressive enhancement in mind. The critical parts of each worked whether or not the transforms, transitions, or animations were present. When present, they added to the experience. When not, everything still worked.

You may have noticed that most of the work and code went into the "making things work" layer. Adding a transition or animation was usually minor in comparison.

Animations and transitions are best used in moderation along with a subtle touch. You aren't creating Disney-length animation, but rather small enhancements that add up to much more.

Use motion to help guide people through the website interface. Use it to help orient visitors, provide cues for what's happening, direct people to important information, and point out areas of the page and site they might want to explore.

Use transforms, transitions, and animation to provide a positive emotional experience and to evoke a positive emotional response. Use motion to communicate more than what a static graphic can communicate.

Trends

Trends come and go. The latest change has been one of moving from skeuomorphic realism to a flatter design aesthetic with little to no use of depth. Designers have been using realistic details to delight viewers, and given the trend to flat aesthetics, something needs to replace them.

What's going to replace skeuomorphic depth are the things you've been learning about in this book. Motion is a good way to add delight to a website. It takes advantage of the strengths of the web. Motion is fluid and dynamic and a perfect match for how your designs will display on screen.

Motion is already replacing depth on today's websites, and its use will only increase over the next few years. Motion allows elements to interact with each other. The smaller screens of mobile devices leads to designing information that remains hidden until requested and then slides in or scales up or uses a transitional effect.

For years, changes on a website happened abruptly. One moment a button is blue, and the next it's red. Animation softens these changes and brings something organic to a website. Moving elements show where something came from or is going, which can direct the eye through a design. It can establish connections showing that a small element was enlarged after a click and not covered up or replaced. Without the animation connecting the before and after, a viewer could mistakenly think the before and after are composed of different elements.

Motion is a core part of the mobile experience. It's used to create page-turning effects, to reveal and hide information, and to rubberband back in place when scrolling past the end of the page. Interact with your phone or tablet and notice all the things that are animating in some small way.

Next Steps

This book shouldn't be your only visit to the world of transforms, transitions, and animations. What I've presented is relatively easy to understand and use in practice. But much more exists beyond this book.

As you practice, you'll find yourself repeating similar techniques and patterns in your code, your effects, and how you apply effects to a design. Use your imagination and continue to explore. Many websites offer tutorials and examples of effects you can apply to different types of changes.

Practice, practice, practice. If you didn't type the code as you read through each chapter, go back and type it. It's only when you can write the code on your own that you'll be able to master what you've learned and use it in your work. The only way to do that is to practice. Type the examples here or ones you find online or in other books and modify the code. Change values. Try a different transform. Turn a transition into an animation. Experimenting this way is how you can make the code your own.

A book like this can offer you the theory, and it can show you the way. It can't make you drink the water after leading you to it. Practice, practice, practice.

Although the theory and techniques in this book are fairly simple, what's difficult is gaining a sense of how long to make a transition last or how much to rotate an element. The Disney principles can help, but the only way to get this sense is through trial and error and writing code.

Let your imagination, your creativity, and your aesthetic eye guide your exploration and bring you back with a stronger ability to work with transforms, transitions, and animations.

Take advantage of effects others have created or, better yet, build a library of your own effects.

Thanks

Thank you again for reading this book. I hope you've found it valuable. Now explore and let your imagination run free!

RESOURCES

Here are some of the resources I used to write this book and some additional resources I thought you might find useful. They are organized by the chapter and topic to which they are most relevant.

Chapter 1: Introduction

- www.smashingmagazine.com/2010/04/26/designing-for-a-hierarchy-of-needs

- www.vanseodesign.com/web-design/skeuomorphism

- www.vanseodesign.com/web-design/flat-design-done-wrong

- www.vanseodesign.com/web-design/flat-design-new-foundation

Browser Support

- http://caniuse.com

- http://HTML5please.com

- http://mobileHTML5.org

Polyfills

- https://github.com/pbakaus/transformie

- http://paulbakaus.com/2008/08/16/bringing-CSS-transform-to-internet-explorer

- www.useragentman.com/blog/2010/03/09/cross-browser-css-transforms-even-in-ie

Chapter 2: Transforms

- www.w3.org/TR/CSS3-transforms

- www.vanseodesign.com/CSS/transforms

- http://msdn.microsoft.com/en-us/library/ie/hh673529%28v=vs.85%29.aspx

- https://developer.mozilla.org/en-US/docs/Web/CSS/transform

- http://desandro.github.io/3dtransforms

Visual Formatting Model

◆ www.w3.org/TR/CSS21/visuren.html

◆ https://developer.mozilla.org/en-US/docs/Web/Guide/CSS/
Visual_formatting_model

Transform Matrix

◆ http://dev.opera.com/articles/understanding-the-css-transforms-matrix

◆ www.useragentman.com/blog/2011/01/07/
CSS3-matrix-transform-for-the-mathematically-challenged

Chapter 3: Transitions

◆ www.w3.org/TR/css3-transitions

◆ www.vanseodesign.com/css/transitions

◆ www.css3.info/preview/css3-transitions

◆ https://developer.mozilla.org/en-US/docs/Web/CSS/transition

◆ http://blog.alexmaccaw.com/css-transitions

Timing Functions

◆ http://easings.net

◆ http://cubic-bezier.com

◆ https://medium.com/design-ux/bea05243fe3

◆ www.the-art-of-web.com/css/timing-function

◆ www.smashingmagazine.com/2014/04/15/understanding-css-
timing-functions

Transition Events

◆ www.kirupa.com/html5/the_transitionend_event.htm

Animatable Properties

* https://developer.mozilla.org/en-US/docs/Web/CSS/CSS_animated_
properties

* http://leaverou.github.io/animatable

Chapter 4: Animation

* www.w3.org/TR/css3-animations

* www.vanseodesign.com/css/animation

* https://developer.mozilla.org/en-US/docs/Web/CSS/animation

* http://docs.webplatform.org/wiki/css/properties/animations

* www.valhead.com/category/video-tutorial

* http://blog.teamtreehouse.com/css3-animation-demystified

* http://webdesign.tutsplus.com/tutorials/a-beginners-introduction-to-
css-animation--cms-21068

Animation Events

* www.kirupa.com/html5/css_animation_events.htm

Transitions vs. Animations

* www.kirupa.com/html5/css3_animations_vs_transitions.htm

* www.bryanbraun.com/2014/05/05/
css-transitions-vs-keyframe-animations

* http://learn.shayhowe.com/advanced-html-css/transitions-animations

Performance

* www.html5rocks.com/en/tutorials/speed/high-performance-animations

* https://docs.google.com/a/google.com/spreadsheet/pub?key=
0ArK1Uipy0SbDdHVLc1ozTFlja1dhb25QNGhJMXN5MXc&single=
true&gid=0&output=html

◆ http://blogs.adobe.com/webplatform/2014/03/18/css-animations-and-transitions-performance

◆ http://csstriggers.com

Chapter 5: More Realistic Animation

◆ www.amazon.com/Disney-Animation-The-Illusion-Life/dp/0896592324

◆ www.amazon.com/Drawn-Life-Classes-Stanchfield-Lectures/dp/0240810961

◆ www.amazon.com/Drawn-Life-Classes-Stanchfield-Lectures/dp/0240811070

◆ www.animationmeat.com/pdf/misc/waltstanchfield/22ws_dwng_principles.pdf

Disney's 12 Principles of Animation

◆ http://atec.utdallas.edu/midori/Handouts/Principles.pdf

◆ www.dgp.toronto.edu/~patrick/csc418/notes/tutorial11.pdf

◆ https://courses.cs.washington.edu/courses/cse459/12au/exercises/animation_principles.html

◆ www.87seconds.com/en/video-marketing-blog/read/the-12-basic-principles-of-stunning-animation-video

◆ www.digitalartsonline.co.uk/features/illustration/12-rules-of-animation

◆ http://johnkcurriculum.blogspot.com/2009/12/disney-principles.html

◆ http://the12principles.tumblr.com

◆ http://floatlearning.com/2013/06/applying-the-principles-of-animation-to-css3-animations-part-1

◆ http://floatlearning.com/2013/06/applying-the-principles-of-animation-to-css3-animations-part-2

◆ http://floatlearning.com/2013/07/applying-the-principles-of-animation-to-css3-animations-part-3

- www.smashingmagazine.com/2011/09/14/the-guide-to-css-animation-principles-and-examples
- http://vimeo.com/74033738
- http://vimeo.com/93206523

Applying Animation Principles to User Interface Design

- http://hci.stanford.edu/courses/cs448b/papers/Chang_AnimationInUI_UIST93.pdf
- https://medium.com/@pasql/transitional-interfaces-926eb80d64e3
- http://alistapart.com/article/ui-animation-and-ux-a-not-so-secret-friendship
- http://alistapart.com/article/web-animation-at-work
- www.beyondkinetic.com/motion-ui-design-principles
- https://medium.com/p/3d1b0a9b810e

Chapter 6: Examples

- http://tympanus.net
- http://codepen.io
- http://lea.verou.me
- http://sarasoueidan.com
- www.valhead.com

Effects

- http://daneden.github.io/animate.css
- www.josebrowne.com/open/tutorial-easy-css-animations-with-animate-css
- http://webdesign.tutsplus.com/tutorials/quick-tip-bring-your-website-to-life-with-animatecss--cms-19423

- http://h5bp.github.io/Effeckt.css
- http://ianlunn.github.io/Hover
- http://projects.lukehaas.me/css-loaders
- http://tympanus.net/Development/SidebarTransitions
- http://tympanus.net/Development/ItemTransitions
- http://tympanus.net/Development/ModalWindowEffects

Index

D

decelerating transitions. *See* accelerating/decelerating transitions
delaying
  animations, 125–127
  transition starts, 79–81
depth cues, 4–5
detecting browser support, 95
Disney Animation (Johnston and Thomas), 148
Disney, Walt, 148–149
Drawn to Life (Stanchfield and Hahn), 208
drop-down menu for navigation bar, 218–223
duration of transitions, 66–68

E

easing
  ease curves, 74
  ease-in curves, 76, 107–111
  ease in/out animation principle, 182
  ease-in-out curves, 78
  ease-out curves, 77
effects. *See also* transforms; transitions
  resources on, 296–297
elements. *See also* child elements; pseudo-elements
  adding multiple transforms to, 29–30
  applying multiple transitions to, 62–63, 92
  delaying start of transitions, 79–81
  moving to different location, 21–22
  numeric values when making smaller, 23
  scaling, 22–23
  setting transition duration for, 66–68
  step functions for timing transitions in, 69–71
  translating to different location, 21–22, 52
ending animations, 105, 132, 139
environment for staging, 164–165
event listeners
  adding for animation events, 137, 138, 139–140
  adding JavaScript, 84
  setting up for content switcher, 273–275
events
  buttons triggering animation, 123–125
  listening for animation, 136, 137–138, 139–140
  resources on, 293, 294
  transitions firing, 84, 92
  types of animation, 131–140
exaggeration, 197–206
example code. *See also* bounce animation; *and specific examples*
  content switcher, 269–285
  how to use, 212–213
  modal windows, 224–241
  navigation bar, 213–223

off-canvas sidebar navigation, 242–268
squash and stretch, 150–158

F

Flash animation, 7
`flat` value for `transform-style` property, 39
follow-through, 168–181
forms, 227–228
functions
  cubic Bézier curves, 69, 72–78
  distinguishing 2-D and 3-D, 52
  `matrix()`, 25–28
  `matrix3d()`, 53–54
  `rotate()`, 23, 52
  `scale()`, 22–23, 52
  `skew()`, 24
  step, 69–71
  3-dimensional, 52–54
  `translate()`, 21–22, 52
  2-dimensional transform, 21–28
  using multiple transform, 29–30

H

Hahn, Don, 208
hiding/showing
  front card face, 46
  previously defined `@keyframes` rule, 103
  submenu with opacity, 219–221
hovering
  adding `animation-name` to elements in `:hover` state, 106
  changing background color when, 60–61, 63–65
  reversing transitions when removed, 91–93
HTML
  animation using dynamic, 6–7
  code for modal windows, 225–226
  drop-down menu code in, 218
  setting up content switcher document in, 269–270
  structuring off-canvas sidebar navigation, 243–246, 260–261

I

icons for menu items, 247
IE (Internet Explorer)
  converting CSS transforms to filters in, 13
  transitions using, 58
  `window.getComputedStyle` workaround for, 256
  workarounds for `inline-block` method, 216
  workaround for `preserve-3d`, 42

inheritance for `transform-origin` property, 18–19
`inline-block` method, 215–216

J

JavaScript
  adding event listeners, 84
  animation using, 7
  changing `animation-name` property for
    off-canvas sidebar, 254–257
  converting transforms to IE filters with, 13
  examples used in transform code, 14
  finding libraries for animation, 95–96
  listening for animation events, 137, 138, 139–140
  polyfills for unsupported CSS, 7–9
  transitions and ease of control in, 142
  usefulness of, 288
  using animations in CSS or, 96
Johnston, Ollie, 148
jQuery, 95

K

keyframes. *See also* `@keyframes` rule
  animation, 94
  applying `animation-timing-function`
    between, 107
  creating anticipation with, 158–164
  defined, 101
  defining with `@keyframes` rule, 101–104
  overriding timing functions in, 111, 113, 114
  placement of transitions and animations in, 142
  resetting property values in, 100
  setting up timing with, 197
keywords
  `all`, 62
  `animation-fill-mode`, 128
  Bézier curve, 73, 74–78
  `perspective-origin`, 37
  `transform-origin`, 17

L

layers of design needs, 2–3, 288
laying out pages, 143–145
length values in `perspective` property, 34
libraries for JavaScript animation, 95–96
linear curves, 75
links for navigation bar, 214–217
list items
  adding for drop-down menu, 218
  displaying horizontally, 215
  selecting, 215–216

looping
  animations, 114–118, 142, 143
  unavailable with transitions, 142

M

matrix math, 25–26, 29
`matrix()` function, 25–28
`matrix3d()` function, 53–54
measurements in `translate()` function, 22
mobile device navigation, 243
modal windows, 224–241
  adding card flip to, 234–235, 236
  code for opening/closing overlay, 229–231
  container and button code for, 226–227
  debate over, 224
  form labels for, 227–228
  HTML code for, 225–226
  illustrated, 224–225
  moving offscreen, 232–234
  scaling to final size, 236–237
  setting color and opacity for, 228–229
  shrinking, 237–239
  using multiple transitional effects in, 239–240
motion. *See* animation
moving elements to different location, 21–22
`ms` vendor prefix, 5, 13
multiple animations, 100

N

naming transform property, 16
navigation. *See* navigation bar; off-canvas sidebar
  navigation
navigation bar, 213–223
  drop-down menu for, 218–223
  illustrated, 213
  links for, 214–216
  selecting list items from, 215–216
  setting background color for, 216–217
  setting up horizontal elements for, 215
nested transforms, 28
numbers
  about matrices, 25–26
  values for making elements smaller, 23

O

objects
  applying principle of solid drawing to, 206–207
  arcs and motion of, 182–183
  rotating around axis, 23
  setting origin of transformed, 16–20